BRIAN LINFORD
PRESENTS...
THE
MARDI-GRAS CLUB LIVERPOOL

THE FAMOUS AND LEGENDARY JAZZ CLUB

Typeset in Adobe Jenson Pro

Editing, design, typesetting and publishing by UK Book Publishing

www.ukbookpublishing.com

ISBN: 978-1-912183-31-9

Contents

Mardi Gras building 1951 painting by Alan P. Tankard from a book by Kay Parrot 'Portrait of Liverpool'. (Bluecoat Press.)

Mardi Gras Club, Liverpool by Brian Linford

The Opening

The *Melody Maker*, a national newspaper dedicated to the music scene, reported, in the 18th October 1958 issue:

'Liverpool's most ambitious jazz project, the Mardi Gras Club, opens on October 30th with a session by the full Johnny Dankworth Orchestra. The club's premises, a former billiard hall in Mount Pleasant, has been decorated in ultra-modern style and will have sessions five nights a week.'

The Mardi Gras Jazz Club opened on Thursday 30th October 1958. The club, in Mount Pleasant in the centre of Liverpool, was owned by two local businessmen, Stan Roberts and Jimmy Ireland. That night it featured the Johnny Dankworth Orchestra plus local band Chris Hamilton's Jazzmen.

Friday 31st October. Ken Collier's (sic) Jazzmen played supported by The Druids Jazz Band Saturday 1st November. Kenny Ball's Jazzmen, plus local band 'Bags Watmough' with singer Jackie Lynn.

Liverpool Echo, 30th October 1958

Kenny Ball was playing with clarinettist Terry Lightfoot and his New Orleans Jazzmen. He decided the time was ripe to launch out on his own; he quit Lightfoot together with trombonist John Bennett towards the end of 1958 to form his own band.

The Mardi was one of their first engagements even before their London debut. First recruit to the new band was clarinettist Dave Jones. The 'front-line' of the band remained unchanged for many years; the rhythm section chopped and changed at the beginning but eventually settled down to make steady headway.

Sunday 2nd November Kenny Ball's Jazzmen plus the voice of Muddy Waters with pianist Otis Spann. Muddy was rated one of the world's best blues singers; he and Otis were making their first visit to the UK and extended their tour to include the club.

The club's advertisement for the opening night read "Come and enjoy genuine jazz in luxurious surroundings". It was hoping to become known as the north's No1 jazz centre. Signing Johnny Dankworth had meant weeks of negotiating as Dankworth had shown no interest in club work outside the capital.

The Mardi Gras was the culmination of Stan and Jimmy's long held ambition to have a permanent place for jazz. They had previously tried to promote jazz on a Sunday night at a restaurant, which they owned, 'The Majorca Grill' on Tarleton Street in the city centre.

Both partners were keen to have a club dedicated to live jazz music. A snooker club became available in Mount Pleasant. This was the 'Compton Club'. They had tried a jazz session there for one night only but it was not suitable – problems with the snooker tables and they were not able to have the bar open due to licensing problems. The lease on the premises became available, which Stan and Jimmy secured.

What they had in mind would be the opposite of the Cavern with its underground setting. The owners were determined to build up that section of fans who like their jazz in a less Bohemian atmosphere: the club would be a place of luxury with carpets, a licensed bar, a big stage with a magnificent grand piano and a wooden sprung dance floor. An artist friend of Jimmy's, Bob Percival, painted the backdrop for the stage, with a Liverpool scene; at the sides the windows were covered with hardboard and murals painted of various jazz musicians. The rest of the club was painted with a very dark blue emulsion. The week before the opening, the 'Liverpool Echo' Mersey Beat (Steve Voce) column reported calling into the new club premises. *Next*

Thursday should be a big night for local fans with the opening of the new luxury Mardi Gras Club. Sharing the bill with the Johnny Dankworth Band will be the Chris Hamilton Jazzmen, the local band who are to feature prominently at the club this winter.

When we popped in the other day part-owner Stan Roberts had donned overalls and was directing workmen putting the finishing touches to the new premises.

Magnificent wall murals by local artist Bob Percival of jazzmen in action and three dimensional stage background looks like adding up to the right kind of atmosphere. The only bright lights were on the stage, bar, toilets and cloakrooms.

Saturday 1st November 'Jazzman' reported in the 'Liverpool Echo': "this should be one of the busiest post-war winters in the Liverpool jazz scene. With the Cavern determined to hold its following for jazz in an underground setting and the Mardi Gras determined to build up the section of fans who like their jazz in a less bohemian atmosphere. There will be a galaxy of bands on view. The Mardi Gras has booked the Yorkshire Jazz Band, The Saints and Dizzy Burton's Jazz Aces for next weekend, and will follow up with visits from Wally Fawkes' Troglodytes and the Dill Jones Trio. The Cavern brings the Vic Ash Band next Thursday and for following weeks has booked Acker Bilk, Mick Mulligan, Alex Welsh and Terry Lightfoot. It will be an interesting test of the size of the jazz following in this city to see if both clubs are packed when they each feature a London band on the same night.

"Nothing is more demographic than the jazz world, millionaires' sons mingle with the artisans in gatherings of the fans when a famous jazz group hits town and the colour bar, like the Russian Sputnik, is something talked about but rarely seen in action. On Thursday night at the successful opening of the Mardi Gras Club we saw Johnny Dankworth, who earlier this year refused a highly paid South African tour for his band because of his feelings on the colour bar there. He is a member of the Anti-Colour bar committee set up by London musicians this year; so are Mick Mulligan and his Liverpool born singer George Melly.

George Worrall and his pal 'Chick' Burgess attended the first night and became regulars for many years."

The capacity of the club was 600. The members were able to listen, dance and have a drink in pleasant surroundings. The club considered itself to be unique in having a licensed bar. The owners also wanted to encourage local musicians to join in a free 'Jam' session.

As you entered the club from street level the doormen would check your membership card. Non-members were required to write their name and address in the visitors' book; a member also counter signed alongside the visitor's entry. Visitors were then warned they must not attempt to buy drinks from the bar – only members had that privilege.

Up two short flights of stairs and the cash desk on the right side, visitors paid an extra 1/- (5 pence) on top of the admission prices which varied each night.

Two of the doormen were members of the Corps of Commissioners, both in uniform.

Jim Wilson was one of those doormen; he also worked in the reception area at Liverpool Football Club on match days. Jim was very popular and well liked; he remained at the Mardi for many years.

As you entered the club the stage was immediately to your left. The snack bar was straight ahead with the licensed bar on the left hand side. The band room was quite spacious with a full size snooker table; visiting bands arriving early appreciated a game of snooker before going on stage. The bar sold draught bitter in half-pint glasses and the usual bottle beers, spirits and soft drinks, all supplied by a family brewery, Cunningham's of Warrington.

Immediately in front of the stage on the dance floor were two rows of 20 wooden chairs for members who just wanted to listen. Tables and chairs were also placed by the walls. Joan Aiello (Murrow) worked at the club with her friend Maureen, on the cash desk or behind the snack bar, their full time employment being GPO telephonists. Among the celebrities Joan remembers in particular were Jimmy Tarbuck and Liverpool and Everton footballers.

Jimmy Currie recalls playing snooker there during his lunch break at the billiard club; he was a student at nearby Clarence Street College, and he then became a jazz club member attending sessions for many years.

Former band leader Harry Ormesher became the club's first manager. Former professional boxer Alan Tanner worked at the club as a doorman/handyman.

The second week the club management announced two important signings.

The Bags Watmough Band signed a contract to play at the club for the next twelve months. Jimmy Rushing, when appearing at the Cavern, was backed by the Bags Watmough Band, Jimmy commenting that the band reminded him of Basie. His (Bags') quiet manner belies his capacity to rave. Bags, his nickname, comes from his early addiction to a jazz tune called 'Bags Grove', a jazz album by Miles Davis

This was followed by the biggest surprise, the signing of the Dill Jones Trio to commence 22nd November. They would be the resident trio and this agreement was quite a scoop: they were currently resident trio on ITV Sunday Break. Dill Jones was born in the same Welsh village as poet Dylan Thomas.

Tuesday 4th November featured a 'Jam' session. This was an open session which any musician could 'sit-in'.

Tuesday night became a feature of the club for many years; it was free to members and on the first night 300 people attended.

The singer with Bags' band, Jackie Lynn, received rave reviews, and by the end of the month she had received offers to sing with two London bands plus a TV appearance.

Jackie, a 25 year old Southport housewife, was formerly a vocalist with the Bill Gregson Band. She once sat in for a session with the Mick Mulligan Band and their high opinion of her as a jazz vocalist made her decide to cut out pops and concentrate on our kind of music. "Bags thinks she's great and should build up a big following in the Merseyside clubs."

The Tuesday 'Jam' sessions proved a great success with musicians on one night from the Merseysippi Jazz Band, Bags Watmough, Chris Hamilton, and Wall City Jazzmen, with the highlight on one of these occasions being the playing of ex Teddy Foster tenor saxophone Jimmy Thompson.

Bags and the Chris Hamilton Jazzmen were the two resident bands appearing twice a week. They supported visiting bands, The Saints, The Jazz Aces, Wally Fawkes' Troglodytes, and Kenny Baker. The club opened five nights a week, closing on Monday and Wednesday.

Early December saw the return of Kenny Ball's Jazzmen on Friday 5th and Sunday 7th.

The club was closed on Saturday 6th for a private function.

The following week Wally Fawkes' Trogs were back for a weekend double, Friday 11th and Sunday 13th. The Humphrey Lyttleton 15 was playing at the Empire Theatre on the Sunday night. After the show they came along to the club. Keith Christie, Eddie Harvey and Johnny Pickard sat in with the 'Trogs' and 'blew a storm'. Sunday 20th December the club debut of the Fairweather-Brown All Stars

– Sandy Brown (clarinet) and Al Fairweather (trumpet) who had met in 1944 as students at Art College in Edinburgh.

Wednesday 24th December, Christmas Eve, Bags Watmough with Jackie Lynn and Chris Hamilton's Jazzmen.

Christmas Day the club was closed.

Friday 26th December, Boxing Day, Alan Pendlebury's Jazzmen plus Bags Watmough Band.

Saturday 27th December the Bruce Turner Band appear for the first time, supported by the Dill Jones Trio.

Sunday 28th December Bruce Turner Band are joined by Kenny Baker on trumpet.

Wednesday 31st December, New Year's Eve, Crescent Jazz Band plus The Druids bring in the New Year.

It has been reported elsewhere that the Mardi Gras opened on 28th September 1957. This is not correct. At that time Jimmy and Stan owned a restaurant 'The Majorca' in Tarleton Street in the city centre. With the success of the Cavern Club the partners decided there was room for another jazz club, and sessions were held on a Sunday evening featuring among others Chris Hamilton Jazzmen, The Dark Town Skiffle (one of the groups Ringo Starr played for) and The Pilgrims Skiffle Group.

When the building in Mount Pleasant became available, Jimmy and Stan grasped the chance, the result being the world famous Mardi Gras Jazz Club.

Central Hall (Mardi Gras) late 1890s

Licensing Hours.
31. Excisable liquors shall only be supplied in the Club during such hours as the General Committee (with the approval of the Proprietor) shall from time to time determine and until such determination shall be made, during the following hours.

Weekdays   ...   12 noon to 1 p.m.
                         3 p.m. to 10 p.m.

Sundays, Christmas Day,
& Good Friday   12 noon to 2 p.m.
                         7 p.m. to 10 p.m.

32. No unlawful game or wagering on any pretext be carried on in the Club. Any breach of this rule shall entitle the General Committee to exercise the powers conferred upon it by **Rule 19.**

Page from Mardi Gras rule book

CERTIFICATE OF REGISTRATION

I hereby Certify that a Statement of particulars furnished by

Roberts & Ireland Limited

in the name of

MARDI GRAS CLUB

of:-   19, Mount Pleasant, Liverpool, 1

pursuant to Sections 3 & 4 _____ of the above-mentioned Act

was registered on the 29th day of October 19 58

Dated this 4th day of November 19 58

Registrar of Business Names.

Section 6 of the Act enacts that, if a change occurs in any of the particulars registered, such change must be notified to the Registrar on the prescribed form within 14 days of its occurrence. The Board of Trade may, on application, allow an extension of the period within which such notification must be made.

Section 13 as amended enacts that, if a firm, individual or company, registered under the Act ceases to carry on business, the partners of the firm, the individual (or if he is dead his personal representative), or the directors or liquidators of a company, must give notice thereof to the Registrar on the prescribed form, within three months after the business has ceased.

Section 18 enacts that all trade catalogues, trade circulars, showcards and business letters bearing the business name and issued by a firm or individual registered under the Act shall clearly state the Christian names or initials and the present surname, any former Christian names or surname, of each partner or individual, together with his nationality, if not British. If a Corporation is a partner its corporate name must this applies to the documents mentioned.

Section 16 require that Certificates issued under the Act must be kept exhibited in a conspicuous position at the principal place of business.

Business name registration

11

Merseysippi Jazz Band

Merseysippi Jazz Band 1954. (L to R) John Lawrence, Pete Daniels, George Bennett, Dick Goodwin, Frank Robinson, Don Lydiatt, Frank Parr, Ken (Nob) Baldwin

My involvement with the Liverpool music scene started in 1953. A neighbour, George Bennett, played drums with the 'Merseysippi Jazz Band' (MJB); I would help him to carry his drum kit in to the city centre. We travelled on the number 33 tram, from Aigburth Road to Lord Street and walked 500 yards to the Temple restaurant in Dale Street. The MJB played there every Sunday night and called it the 'West Coast Jazz Club'; the famous actor Liverpool-born Derek Guylar was the club President. Derek would occasionally 'sit-in' with the band playing washboard. The rest of the band 'line-up' included Pete Daniels and John Lawrence (trumpets), Frank Parr (trombone), Don Lydiatt (clarinet), Dick Goodwin (bass), Frank Robinson (piano) and Ken (Nob) Baldwin (banjo). Frank Parr was also well known as the wicket-keeper for Lancashire County Cricket Club and at one time he was considered for a place in the England Test Team.

The entrance to the room upstairs was via a stone staircase. There was another stairway inside the room which led down to the bar on the ground floor. The room held about 100 people all seated and attendances were growing weekly. Vinnie Attwood, who looked after the door, taking money, and handing out membership forms, was so busy that I volunteered my services. It was not long before the doors were closed at 8pm, club capacity having been reached.

The management at the Temple restaurant obtained the premises next door, which were at ground level. The band moved into the new room, which could hold 200 people, again an all seated audience and no dancing, the new entrance being in Dale Street. Once again the popularity of the Sunday night sessions continued until it got to the point where if you were not in the queue by 7pm you wouldn't get in. With the success of the club three new members of the door staff from the Corps of Commissioners were engaged, one of them being a retired Sergeant Major who assumed command. After a short while he started to question the dress code of the members, especially the men. He would refuse them entry for wearing jeans or drain-pipe trousers. Dick Goodwin asked him to be more tolerant towards members; he didn't alter and was asked to leave. Picton Hall, just down the road in William Brown Street, promoted Sunday night jazz sessions presenting well known London jazz bands; even this competition didn't affect attendance at the Temple. The MJB did play at the 'Picton' one Friday evening in support of former Benny Goodman Trio pianist Teddy Wilson. Wilson made a request for George Bennett to accompany him on drums and even though this put his musician union membership at risk, and without any rehearsal, George readily agreed. Wilson thanked George and congratulated him on his performance. Shortly after this gig George left the band to be replaced by Trevor Carlisle.

With the bigger room at the Temple, the band needed a sound system; this was supplied by Charlie McBain. Charlie organised dances at Garston swimming baths. The large pool was not used during the winter so it was covered over with boards. He eventually had permanent premises across the road when they built Wilson Hall.

One of the MJB highlights during this period was a concert featuring the 'Louis Armstrong All Stars' at the old Liverpool boxing stadium. They were invited to play as support band. The boxing ring was a revolving stage. I had a seat on the front row (ringside). At one point 'All Stars' trombonist Trummy Young came off the stage and sat on the front row seat opposite me and continued to play. All the photographers got behind him to take their 'shots', the result being a magnificent photograph of Trummy with myself in the background. The photograph along with others taken at the concert appeared on display in a shop window in Manchester Street – the photographer was Peter Kaye. I met Trummy a few years later and he signed the photograph. I was introduced to Louis after the concert in his dressing room and shook hands with him; a truly magic moment.

Trummy Young (trombone) with the Louis Armstrong
All Stars at Liverpool Boxing Stadium 20th May
1956. Brian Linford (striped socks) front row

Merseysippi Jazz Band with Louis Armstrong,
Liverpool Boxing Stadium, 20th May 1956

The Cavern Club

The Cavern Club, 1958

December 1956 I was told about a possible move by the MJB from the Temple to new premises in nearby Mathew Street. Charlie McBain and I went along to this new club during the interval at the Temple. The place was a cellar and it was in a bit of mess considering it would be opening in five weeks. The new club would be called

'The Cavern'. Mathew Street ran parallel with Victoria Street which housed mainly warehouses used by the wholesale fruit trade; the 'Cavern' premises had at some time been used for this purpose.

The Merseysippi Jazz Band (MJB) decided to move from the Temple and give their support to 'The Cavern' and the owner Alan Sytner. The initial success of 'The Cavern' I would say was due to the tremendous popularity and following of the MJB.

The 'Cavern' opened on Wednesday 16th January 1957. A crowd of 2000 people turned up that night with the queue stretching down Mathew Street and into Whitechapel – most were disappointed the club had room for only 600. The MJB was the first band to play at the club. I couldn't attend the opening night as I had two more weeks of my National Service to complete, although I could get home every weekend. I worked on the door with Vinnie Attwood on Friday 18th, Saturday 19th and Sunday 20th. The following weekend I worked the same three days. After my demob, on 30th January, I was at the club every night. One of the features was the entrance: the very narrow stone steps were in a straight line into the club. After a couple of weeks they were altered so that you went down about 10 steps, there was of a square of about four feet, and then a left turn down three steps into the club. You were then met by three people, sitting at a desk, including myself, taking money or handing out membership forms.

The club consisted of three archways about 75 feet long; each archway, which was about 10 feet wide, had an arched opening about six feet wide and the 'pillars' were about two feet wide.

You passed the desk as you entered and turned left; straight ahead was a snack bar and cloakroom. In the centre arch at the top there were huge iron gates, behind which was the hoist that had been used in the past to lower goods into the cellar. These gates were permanently locked and at times used as a store room. This middle arch also had an entrance to the ladies' and gents' toilets. The next arch had a cloakroom. All these services were at the top end of the club. The opposite end, in the middle, there was the stage, and 50 wooden seats in front of the stage. To the left, behind a wooden structure, was the band room, which had a simple wooden door with just a latch and without a security lock. The arch to the right eventually had an extra cloakroom built. The decoration was very sparse and the floor just had the original bricks which were in places quite uneven.

When the club was packed, which would be often, the heat was stifling and the condensation would run down the walls. When musicians came into the club they had a struggle to get to the band room passing many sweaty bodies.

The snack bar sold Coca-Cola, coffee and hot dogs. The first manager, Ricky Ashun, was appointed a few weeks after opening. It wasn't long before all the 'desk-staff' were replaced by the staff from Alan Sytner's accountants including Ray McFall. I had odd jobs around the club but nothing permanent until a late night visit by 'Fat Harold', a well-known local thug. He came into the club with two of his cronies, just on closing time. Alan told them to get out and immediately received a thump from Harold; uproar ensued trying to get the three assailants off the premises, which was not easy in a basement situation. The result being I was reinstated as a member of the door staff.

With the poor lighting in the club I was often mistaken for Alan, being about the same age, size and shape. A lad came up to me in the club praising the medical skill of my father (Dr Sytner) and how he had saved the life of his mother. I didn't have the heart to say you've got the wrong person, so I told him I was pleased to hear about his mother's improving health.

The club started to have lunchtime sessions, which proved a great attraction. I remember Alma Cogan coming into club during one of these sessions; she wore a large pair on sunglasses and dressed as if she had a dinner date – I don't think she wanted to be noticed but she stuck out like a sore thumb.

The music was all traditional jazz featuring mainly local bands and at the weekends well known bands from London. When Lonnie Donegan recorded 'Rock Island Line' it became the start of the skiffle era. Lonnie had been playing banjo with the Chris Barber Band. Rock Island Line got to number one in the record charts and he left the band to form his own skiffle group, appearing mainly in variety shows. He held a fan club meeting at the Cavern and brought along with him a young comedian, Des O'Connor. They were appearing in a show at the Liverpool Empire Theatre.

It was not long before a Skiffle Group competition was held at the Cavern because of the huge interest in this type of music. The management started the competition on a Wednesday night. The band room side of the club had as many as 10 tea-chest basses lined up ready to perform with their group. This indeed was the beginning of the 'Mersey Beat' as many of these groups went on to fame and big fortunes, including a group called the 'Quarrymen' featuring John Lennon and Paul McCartney.

The MJB were having a problem in the band room: when they came off stage after a session, the room would be full of people who had no good reason to be there. The band manager Dick Goodwin, wanting a quick exit to the Beaconsfield pub in Victoria Street, was prevented by all these people. He gave me the job of band room doorman. Only guests of the band were allowed into the room. Ringo Starr visited the band room when the 'Darktown Skiffle Group' appeared, having played with them before leaving to join 'Rory Storm'. Ringo and I had something in common. In 1940 I lived in the Dingle at 23 Kinmel Street, adjacent to Madryn Street where three month old Ringo lived. On Saturday 19th October 1940 a German bomb landed on our outside toilet but didn't explode. The whole area was cleared; many people, including Ringo, luckily survived the heavy bombing that night. My family didn't return to that house again due to all the damage, and we were re-housed in nearby Aigburth.

In September 1958 Alan was absent from the club quite a lot. His dad 'Doc' Sytner offered me and a friend Peter Tushingham (brother of Rita), the opportunity of taking over the snack bar and the cloakrooms for a weekly rental of £10 per week to include gas and electric. We both agreed to this arrangement to commence the first week in October. It would be a 'gentlemen's agreement' for a period of six months. Peter and I both worked in the snack bar and we had a 'pool' of six girls who worked in the Cloakrooms.

MJB drummer Trevor Carlisle recalls how he enjoyed a 'fry-up' prepared by Brian and Peter, eggs, bacon and sausages just what he needed after playing two sessions in the hot and sweaty club atmosphere.

Trevor was one of the first musicians to play at the lunchtime session which included John Lawrence, Tommy Smith, Ron McKay, and Red Carter, who were all regulars.

The lunchtime sessions didn't take place during the time that we ran the snack bar.

The club operated on four nights, having dropped the Wednesday session; Thursday featured modern jazz, Friday, Saturday and Sunday traditional jazz with the six piece Blue Genes playing most nights. At the end of October another jazz club opened, the 'Mardi Gras' in Mount Pleasant just ½ mile away. The opinion at the Cavern was positive: it would not affect the attendance, the Cavern being well established; the 'Mardi' having a licensed bar would have trouble with drunkenness and underage drinking etc.

But attendances started to drop and by the end of November especially on Thursdays and Fridays. Christmas night we were the only club of our type open. It was a Thursday, modern jazz night, featuring Alan Branscombe; the attendance was very poor and this caused the management to drop modern jazz, after the Vic Ash 'gig' on New Year's Day and for the future to close on a Thursday .

January 1959 the crowd numbers continued to drop. Someone had the bright idea of having BINGO on a Saturday night. The 'Harlequin Ballroom' (over Burtons) in Church Street had been running bingo sessions with some success. Marcus Nagley called the Cavern bingo. The bingo tickets, or rather boards, were 12" square, with little windows that you closed over the numbers as they were called, the prize being a record player. The bingo lasted for four weeks and then they gave it up as a 'bad job'.

I cannot recall bingo ever being played at the club again.

In March the nights were reduced to just Saturday and Sunday, our rent being adjusted accordingly to £5 per week. The advertisement in the 'Liverpool Echo' Friday 6th March stated 'Closed Tonight for Alterations' – it was closed Fridays for the next couple of weeks. The so called 'alterations' did not take place. Rickie Ashun, who had managed the club for two years, left during this period. At the beginning of March 'The Doc' made Peter and I an offer similar to our snack bar agreement to take over the club entirely. After some consideration, without asking how much would be required in rent, we declined his offer and at the same time told him we didn't wish to continue with the snack bar. We both felt that the Cavern was doomed and had no future, and having full time jobs we didn't think it worth taking the risk. Peter worked in the family grocery business with shops in Hunts Cross and Garston while I worked as a wireman at ATE (later to be called Plessey's) at their factory in Lord Nelson Street in the city centre. Working in the city centre enabled me to visit the club during my lunch break, especially on a Thursday and Friday to make sure deliveries had been completed.

We had an arrangement with a man who worked next door at number 8 to accept deliveries of bread rolls and Coca-Cola. With Peter working in the food trade his shop supplied some provisions and damaged tins of salmon at very reasonable rates.

Spencer Leigh, commenting in his book 'The Cavern' said, 'although the club had started successfully, it was running into trouble, skiffle had lost its novelty appeal. Modern jazz had only an elitist following and trad fans were moving to the newer and plusher Mardi Gras, not to mention the Merseysippis themselves'.

When I was told that Ray McFall had acquired the club, I thought he was taking a big gamble.

I didn't visit the 'Cavern' again until 23rd July 1966. The club had been closed since February of that year and it was the grand re-opening. The Prime Minister, Harold Wilson, unveiled a plaque to commemorate the occasion. Among the VIPs present were MP Bessie Braddock, Ken Dodd, and Jimmy Savile. I received an invitation to the mid-morning event as a special guest. The first group on stage that day were the 'Hideaways'. There was a buffet reception in the new office suite upstairs but I didn't stay – I had a ticket for North Korea v Portugal World Cup quarter-final being played that afternoon at Goodison Park.

It has been reported elsewhere that the Cavern had a smell of rotten fruit and it was quite common to see rats. I spent many hours in the club on my own when it was empty, and it did not smell of any rotting vegetation and I didn't see a rat or any other vermin, and there was no evidence of any mouse 'droppings'.

The Cavern closed due to demolition of the building in May 1973. When the site was developed years later, a very poor replica Cavern Club opened in 1984. The only similarity with the original was its basement setting and being on the same side of the street, but I suppose for the sake of the tourist trade it's acceptable.

Alan Sytner standing left, Jimmy Leech seated right, in the Grapes pub, Mathew Street

Jimmy Leech centre, Neil English right with friend, Cavern Club 1957

The Building

*Mardi Gras 1965. At number 25 Mount Pleasant
there is a large brass sign 'H.Proctor Phrenologist'*

Mount Pleasant in Liverpool city centre has two outstanding landmarks. At the bottom in Ranelagh Place is the famous Adelphi Hotel; as you proceed up the steep incline at the top is the Roman

Catholic Metropolitan Cathedral of 'Christ the King', known to some locally as 'Paddy's Wigwam'. The road also has a number of small hotels and B&B accommodation. The office for the registration of births, deaths and marriages was situated mid-way up the road; it was here that John Lennon married his first wife, Cynthia, on 23rd August 1962.

MP William Roscoe (1753-1831) was born and grew up at the Bowling Green Inn, Mount Pleasant. He was the anti-slave trade campaigner. There is a plaque dedicated to Roscoe in a small garden area just across the road from the 'Mardi' site where he is buried.

The club premises at number 19 was built as a Wesleyan chapel in 1790. John Wesley commented in 1789, "It's a bold step to think of building Mount Pleasant to cost £1100; but go on". In 1889 it was handed over to the Wesleyan mission and became Central Hall. The new Central Hall (Charles Garrett Memorial) in nearby Renshaw Street opened in 1905; the Mount Pleasant building was sold and became a billiard hall.

In 1908 there was another change of use – this time as a cinema; on 14th December that year it opened as the 'New Century Picture Hall', the first organised cinema in the city centre. The comfortable new cinema with a first floor stadium type auditorium was reached by a stairway from Mount Pleasant. The local press reported an auspicious opening at which a large audience expressed enthusiastic admiration for the decorations and well-arranged seating. The proprietors were 'The New Century Animated Picture Co', with managing director Sydney H. Carter. It seated 700 and the grand opening of Liverpool's new hall of entertainment featured 'The Destruction of Hyderabad' with supporting pictures and songs with piano accompaniment. Twice daily, 3pm and 8pm, admission prices 3p, 6p, and 1/-, change of pictures weekly.

In 1915 the cinema came under joint ownership with Lime Street Picture House Co, and continued until 1928 when it was among many cinemas taken over by Denman Picture Houses Ltd, associated with Gaumont British. It re-opened 28th December 1928 as 'The Century Theatre'. The company gave it an entirely new image as the first repertory cinema in the provinces, styled as 'The Home of Unusual Films', rare continental films including 'The Waltz Dream', Fitz Lang's 'Dr. Mabuse' and Emil Jannings in 'Faust' and 'Laugh Clown Laugh', but with 'talkies' coming to Liverpool in 1929 the support of the public was insufficient and the cinema closed 15th February 1930, showing the German film 'Conscience' featuring Bernard Goetake.

In October that year the hall came into use as an auction room by Messrs Turner Sons and Smythe. Turners continued to trade there for many years until they moved to their present premises in Roscoe Street.

A room at first floor level supported by four columns was added on the front of the building; this was for the cinema projection room, and it also sheltered the club members queuing in the rain waiting to enter. On the front of this building was a sign 'Mardi Gras Jazz Club', a box sign with multi coloured letters on perspex illuminated by fluorescent strip lights. During a violent storm the perspex was torn away and severely damaged. A few years earlier a restaurant in Manchester Street called the 'Mardi Gras' had closed. Jimmy bought the sign from the owners, his objective at the time being to prevent another business using the name. Jimmy Leech and Donny Lyle (brother-in-law of Jimmy Ireland) carried the sign across town to the club where it was then stored in the old projection room behind the stage. This became the new sign and remained in position until the end in 1972. The other trades occupying the site included a carpet warehouse, a snooker club and, finally on 30th October 1958, the 'Mardi Gras Jazz Club'.

Mardi Gras building as a cinema 1920s

Fruit Machines
(One Armed Bandits)

At the beginning of the 1960s the new gaming act allowed clubs to install fruit machines. The act stated that there must not be any 'private gain'. All the money had to go back for the benefit of the members. Clubs would be able to install two machines; they could buy them 'outright' or, as most preferred, on a rental system.

Stan and Jimmy decided that this would be their next venture. How do you start?

Len McMillian and I had the job of canvassing clubs for this new business.

The rent for one machine would be £8 per week and £12 for two, payment by bankers' standing order. We were given the incentive of earning commission of £5 per machine, no expenses, and to go canvassing in our spare time, unless we were required to attend a club during our own working hours.

We started with the places known to us, church, political and British Legion clubs. At the beginning we were treated like members of the 'Mafia', and quite often told to leave the premises. Gradually as word got around and clubs realised that it was legitimate business, and also how much money a club could take per week, our job became a lot easier. The legal agreement would be for a period of three years; this included maintenance and being 'on call' from 10am to 11pm.

We became agents for Bell Fruit Machines for Merseyside and The Wirral. The agent for Blackpool and the Fylde coast was former Everton Football Club centre forward Ephraim 'Jock' Dodds; he frequently attended meetings at the club. He was a very big man, always smartly dressed, and very pleasant – you were at ease with him in conversation.

As it became harder to find clubs after signing up the obvious and 'scouring' Yellow Pages, I then went to the city licensing office. You were allowed to look at the club register on payment of 1/-(5p). I then made a note of all the clubs that had been missed and the name of the secretary – it was very handy walking into a club and asking for the secretary by his name.

Len and myself would go out 'on-call' to fix any breakdowns – the most common fault being a bent 6d (all the machines operated with 6d). As the business began to expand, there were now more than 100 machines out on site, so it was necessary to employ more staff as Len and I were neglecting our club duties. Eventually the partners employed four mechanics and a foreman. A friend of Jimmy's, Colin Percy, a team mate from Garston Water Polo Club, became the foreman.

I continued to look for new business, but some clubs still resisted. To help break down the resistance it was decided to offer clubs a two weeks' free trial, all money taken would belong to the club. If at the end of two weeks the club said no, the machines would be removed. This only happened on one occasion. One of the ploys the partners used would be to put £10 worth of coins in each cash box (unknown to the club). This helped to boost the takings – they considered this to be a generous donation to the club. When they realised how much money had been taken the agreement was quickly signed. Getting members of a committee to agree and sign a legal document can be very hard work.

The Crosville Bus Company had a canteen for the staff at Liverpool Pier Head which was open from 6am to 11pm. Two machines were placed there on 'trial'. After three days we received a call: both of the machines were out of order, a mechanic reported back – the machines had taken so much money the overflowing excess coins had 'jammed' the works of the machines. This happened twice during the fortnight. At the end of the trial I went along to the canteen, agreement all prepared, only to be told to take them away. I was dumbfounded – bang goes my £10 commission. We were told it was a decision by the company management, the number of conductors 'paying in short' had increased considerably and the management decided to take away the temptation.

One club in South Liverpool resisted for many years and when they finally fell by realising how they could boost their club funds, my commission by then had increased to £100 a site, but most of the clubs by this time had installed two machines.

Some of the clubs I attended for the committees to quiz me about various aspects of the gaming act. A frequently asked question by those members who were still opposed to the introduction of these 'bandits' was about the number of men who could spend all their wages in them and go home to their families penniless. I would usually say that with a betting shop practically on every street corner, the club could help a member; a betting shop wouldn't.

One of the vehicles bought to transport the machines was an old London Hackney black taxi cab. It held three machines and stands. This arrangement would be OK when the cab was loaded, but when empty and stopped in traffic or at red lights it could cause problems with people jumping in the back who had to be made to get out. On one occasion I stopped at traffic lights, and five burly blokes jumped in – how do I explain it looks like a taxi but it's not! They were going to a football match at Everton, so I decided to take a chance. I was going to a job that way and earned a couple of quid for my trouble.

I continued to go out on call now and again until the introduction of the big electric monsters – my servicing stint came to an end and I was able to concentrate on my club duties and other aspects of the business.

Colin, Jimmy and Brian

Pirate Radio

Pirate Radio started in 1964, the first being Radio Caroline North broadcasting from an old passenger ferry MV FREDERICIA moored off the Isle of Man in the Irish Sea. The founder was an Irish-American, Ronan O'Rahilly. The policy would be to play non-stop pop music as opposed to the rather staid BBC Light Programme which broadcast just two hours of pop music a week. In a very short time they built up a very large audience, providing a commercial radio service, the only other of this type being Radio Luxembourg and the Irish Radio Athlone. The reception of these radio stations was not very good most of the time.

Stan and Jimmy, in partnership with Alan Williams ('The Man Who Gave The Beatles Away'), agreed to launch another pirate radio ship.

The two 'Mardi' partners had been thinking of this idea at the same time as Alan so when they learnt about each other's plans they decided to get together. It was reported in the local musical press: 'the biggest and best news we have had since 'The Beatles' made it in the States'.

They issued a press release that the ship, an ex RAF survey vessel of 195 tons and 120 feet in length, had been acquired by Jimmy from somewhere on the south coast for £5000. I did see a photograph of 'a ship', and a number of sea captains coming to the club for an interview. Legal advisers and marine survey people were working out the best place for the ship to be anchored, bearing in mind that it had to be outside the three mile limit. Jimmy stated that "the whole project will cost £50,000 and hope the programmes beam to Manchester, Liverpool, Blackpool and most of the North West. Broadcasting on air for 12 hours there would be a two man crew, one operational and one relief. The ship will be probably be anchored off the Fleetwood coast". The name of the ship had not been settled; names suggested included Radio Red Rose and Radio Blue Angel. "The DJs will be leaders of beat groups like Earl Preston, other DJs are likely to be 'Mersey Beat' editor Bill Harry" who had plenty of experience in this field having broadcast on radio stations to four continents and having compered stage shows for, among others, 'The Beatles' and 'The Searchers'.

One departure from the usual 'Pirate Radio Station', once the programmes were organised, would be the inclusion of news flashes and sports items as well as music. "This is actually an uneconomic proposition at the moment," confessed Jim Ireland. "We are opening this station because we are determined to keep this part of the world in front and leading the beat field. We are not happy about the London drift of so many Liverpool artistes and managers, nor do we see any reason why London should have the monopoly of beat broadcasts."

Jimmy was being pressed by the local media about the progress of the pirate ship, but he would only confirm that "it would commence in early June". With no progress being made by early July, Jimmy told me to arrange a 'script' and records to make a programme on a tape recorder. The recording on a Grundig reel to reel machine was made on a Saturday afternoon in the office at the club. I had the help of Derek Dolman, Jimmy's nephew, who worked in the office as an assistant for the Swinging Blue Jeans fan club. I played the records (45s) of all the local groups who appeared at the 'Mardi', starting with the Swinging Blue Jeans 'Hippy Hippy Shake'; other groups included 'Earl Preston's Realms', 'Cy Tuckers Friars', and 'The Escorts'.

I started by announcing who I was and continued, "This is Radio Red Rose broadcasting on 200 metres on the medium wave from somewhere in the Irish Sea."

I would then introduce the record and Derek would stop the tape, set up the disk on the record player and press the buttons on both machines to start the recording. I gave 'plugs' about the 'Mardi' and the Downbeat', also the Liverpool Show in Wavertree; I booked the groups for the 'Show'. The broadcast was a bit 'ham-fisted' but we got there in the end.

The programme lasted 45 minutes and Jimmy was happy for it to go out on-air. Listeners were told that this was a trial broadcast and invited comments by phone (Royal 3041) at the 'Mardi', or by post. The only publicity about the programme came from my announcements at the club and Bob Wooler at the Cavern on Saturday 11th July.

The broadcast went on air the next day, Sunday 12th July at 11am, the equipment being housed on the 4th floor of a building in Slater Street on the corner of Seel Street. The engineers rigged-up an aerial about 40 feet high on the roof of the building. They then made an announcement as a test and started to play the tape. Jimmy and I drove out as far as Huyton listening to the broadcast, which came over loud and clear.

Later we called into Bert Whalley's 'Gaslight Club' in Cumberland Street. The reporters from the national and freelance press gathered there on a Sunday, the 'Press Club' being closed on that day until 7pm. They had received some information about the broadcast. Jimmy gave them a statement and further details of the ship. "We have just returned from the ship which was anchored in the Irish Sea, it has now sailed to Amsterdam for maintenance work to improve the standard of reception and to sort out 'legal difficulties' but broadcasting should commence full time in about six weeks."

The next day reports appeared in most of the national and local press about the latest pirate ship. We received 50 letters, some commenting that the DJ was crap, plus phone calls to the club. We wanted to know how far the signal had reached, and some of the letters came from Blackpool and North Wales which meant that the equipment was OK and giving a strong signal.

The statement was deliberately misleading because the penalty for illegal broadcasting was heavy and could have led to hefty fines. The venture came to a halt for what reason I was never told. I can only assume it was the capital outlay and the government's intent to stop this type of broadcasting. With the high risk of losing a lot of money it was brought to an end.

The government were not too happy about 'Radio Caroline' taking away so many BBC listeners, the estimated audience being 25 million. They tried many ways to stop pirate radio and in 1967 passed a law 'The Marine Broadcasting Offences Act'. This made it impossible to advertise or receive goods and services from British companies.

With the demise of pirate radio the BBC launched their own POP radio service and on the 30th September 1967 Radio 1 and 2 commenced and eventually many local radio stations were created. Radio Caroline moved to the North Sea off the Dutch coast but did not regain its UK popularity. The Caroline 'Brand' is still available in some form, mainly in the south of England. If it had not been for Ronan O'Rahilly we could still be listening to the staid BBC.

Theatre Club

The Batley Variety Club in Yorkshire opened March 1967. By the end of the year they were presenting top acts and packing the place.

Stan and I discussed the possibilities of finding premises large enough to hold up to 1000 people, creating our own theatre club.

Old cinemas appeared to be the best option but the chances of getting planning permission were limited due to the lack of parking facilities.

We decided to pay a visit to Batley. On a Monday night in February 1968, six members of staff made the journey over to Yorkshire. When we arrived at the purpose built club with its large car park we were suitably impressed. The club had taken just 16 weeks to build and could hold 2000 people. The entrance and reception area was large and well organised. Entering the auditorium we were bowled over by the size and the layout which was magnificent. A large stage with lighting to suit most atmospheres. After the cabaret, the stage was lowered to accommodate space for dancing.

The seating arrangements went up on spacious tiers, with tables and chairs at the front and rear of each tier, allowing plenty of room for the waitress to move easily between tables. Each side of the club had bars extending the full length of the room. With very efficient staff serving customers quickly, the food served was simple chicken and chips in a basket, which was popular at the time.

The main attraction on the night we attended was Frankie Howard, and the place was packed. Stan was convinced – a club packed on a Monday night and with the bars very busy. The next move would be to find a suitable site to build a club with plenty of space for a carpark. I was given the task of finding a piece of land to suit the purpose. I trawled all the Liverpool estate agents and property columns in the local press. A plot of land in the Allerton area of South Liverpool became available. It was situated between the Allerton pub and the railway station. The land had housed a concrete manufacturer and the owner now wanted to sell the land. A price of £15,000 was agreed, subject to planning permission. A piece of land at the rear of the site belonging to British Rail, who agreed to give us a lease, would be used as a carpark for 700 cars.

An architect, Bryan Evans of the Anthony Clarke Partnership, was appointed. The outline planning permission was granted by the City Council. Plans and a model were produced by Bryan and they looked impressive. The shape of the club would be an amphitheatre to hold 2000 people, the estimated cost being £250,000. To finance the building we approached several breweries. The best offer we received was a 50% loan; this being short of Stan's expectations the idea was eventually dropped. I was very disappointed considering all my input. Contingency plans for the building included use as a bingo hall or a supermarket.

I wrote to millionaire show business agent Harold Davison enquiring if he knew of any enterprising impresario who would be interested in this venture – the theatre clubs were certainly taking off at that time. Harold sent a reply: he had mentioned this to a number of his clients but none had shown any interest.

1959

The beginning of the New Year and the Thursday night session stopped. This may have been a coincidence, but the Cavern also dropped the Thursday modern jazz night from their schedule. Cash may have been the possible cause. Most people were paid by cash on Friday and coming just after Christmas money would be in short supply.

A new addition to the Mardi staff was Jimmy Leech. Jimmy was from Yorkshire and after his National Service on a visit to Blackpool met a girl from Liverpool. Jimmy followed her to her home town and they became engaged but there was no happy ending and they parted. Jimmy liked Liverpool and so decided to stay, becoming a bricklayer. He worked in the evening at the Unicorn Club which was owned by Neil English who was well known in the Liverpool club business. The Mardi manager Harry Ormesher had cause to sack a barman whom he'd caught adding water to the vodka. Harry offered Jimmy the job plus accommodation; Harry was already living in the flat. At the start of his employment Jimmy was required to work at Jimmy and Stan's restaurant, the Majorca Grill, to make up his hours – he worked in the kitchen complete in chefs' whites. The flat had two bedrooms, kitchen, bathroom and WC. This part of the building must have been the house when built in 1789; there was a staircase leading down to the ground floor but the door was well and truly sealed. The ground floor of the house was occupied by a firm of commercial window cleaners, who parked their barrows carrying their ladders, in the yard at the side of the building. The business was managed by a Mr Audley, a Tory councillor on the Liverpool City Council.

The regular sessions continued: 'Jam sessions' on Tuesday, Bags Watmough, and Chris Hamilton playing at the weekend with guest London band on Sunday.

On Friday 6th February a new sound, Cha, Cha,
Cha, with Joe Palin and his Cubandos.

Kenny Ball Jazzmen returned on Saturday 7th and Sunday 8th February. A club member named only as Cecil recommended to Kenny that they played 'Samantha' which became the first number one hit for the band.

At a Tuesday night 'Jam' session in March, a young 15 year old schoolboy walked into the club and asked manager Harry Ormersher if he could have a 'blow'. A little sceptically Harry agreed. He watched the youngster confidently pick up a trumpet and plant himself in front of a rhythm section composed of musicians years his senior. I'll give him a couple of numbers and make some tactful excuse, thought Harry. An hour or so later, the young trumpeter, a perspiring Alan Downey, was still blowing hard to the obvious enjoyment of both himself and 500 folk in the club. Listening to his playing we thought that here was a young jazz player who by the time he reaches his twenties may be a superb jazzman. Says Alan: "For years I've collected jazz records especially those of Dizzy Gillespie, and he is the man I use as a model, now I'm sitting in with jazz groups. I love the music but I've no intention of turning professional; my parents have convinced me the uncertainty of the game."

It was reported elsewhere that Rory Storm and The Hurricanes with Ringo Starr on drums made their club debut on Wednesday 25th March. There is no record of this happening, however; also the club closed on this night and it's very doubtful that manager Harry Ormesher would engage this type of group.

Easter weekend, an addition to the Roberts and Ireland Empire, the opening of another 'Mardi Gras Jazz Club' on Saturday 28th March. The venue Queen Street, Rhyl, North Wales. The opening featured the Mick Mulligan Band with George Melly, Easter Sunday 29th Bags Watmough, and Easter Monday 30th Chris Hamilton Jazzmen with singer Jackie Lynn.

The life of this club was short and within a couple of months it closed.

Mick Mulligan Band with George Melly at Mardi Gras Club, Rhyl

Bags Watmough Band at the Mardi Gras Club, Rhyl, 1959

NAPOLEON BONAPARTE. NAME IN CLUB RAID. This was the headline in a local newspaper. The report continues, 'When police raided a seaside jazz club they took away a list of members. One of the names and addresses read: Napoleon Bonaparte, 12 Champs Elysee, Paris. This was said in court when the proprietors of the Mardi Gras Club, Robertson (*sic*) and Ireland Ltd, Tarleton (*sic*) Street, Liverpool were fined a total of £100 on 10 charges of selling intoxicating liquor when not holding a justices' licence. They were ordered to pay £98 costs and the club was struck off the register for 12 months. Stanley Elson of Rhyl, the secretary/manager, was fined a total of £20 on 10 similar charges. Mr Emlyn Hooson, barrister, said the club was completely bogus.

This was a setback especially for Jimmy – it was often said he had the Midas touch. The MJB left the Cavern in the month of April; they had found the audience becoming hostile to their type of music. The band had played there since the opening night, 16th January 1957. The Mardi management wasted no time in signing up the band along with singers Clinton Ford and Jill Martin; they made their debut on Sunday 26th April.

Saturday 9th and Sunday 10th May the
return of Kenny Ball Jazz Band

The first Riverboat Shuffle on board the Mersey ferry Royal Iris on Saturday 23rd May. The bands sailing down the River Mersey that night, Fairweather-Brown All Stars, and the Art Reid Quintet. Tickets 6 shillings (30 pence). The club remained open as usual that night.

Kenny Ball returned to play on Sunday 7th June; the band had recently been acclaimed by the 'Melody Maker' as the greatest. Also appearing that night was singer Beryl Bryden who was always a big attraction, in many ways. The club continued a trad policy, but on Sunday 21st June presented an evening of modern jazz booking the Jazz Couriers led by Tubby Hayes and Ronnie Scott. This would be their one and only appearance; they disbanded in August that year.

Due to an industrial dispute at the Liverpool Echo from 22nd June until 6th August an emergency edition was produced and some advertisements were missing.

Sunday 9th August the Diz Dizley Soho String Quartet makes their debut. Dizley had played guitar with quite a number of jazz bands. The 'Melody Maker' polls made him the best Guitar Player of the year on many occasions.

A charity memorial night was held on Tuesday 11th August for Mike Farren. Mike played trumpet with the Bags Watmough Band, and had died tragically earlier that year.

The bands playing that night included the MJB, Bags, and Chris Hamilton, plus the usual 'Jam' session; there was an admission charge of a half-crown (12½pence).

The local newspaper reporter for the *Daily Herald*, Norman Dickson, wrote in his Saturday 15th August column: Jimmy Leach(*sic*) the 6 feet tall £8 a week bricklayer from Barnsley, Yorkshire, who threw away his hod to chase a dream job. He found it in Liverpool's Mardi

Gras Jazz Club. He can't play a note of music but jazz is his life, so Jimmy, now the catering manager of the club, hears the best jazz bands in the business and says: "I'm the happiest man alive". Harry Ormesher, who runs the Mardi Gras, told me Jimmy won medals for jiving, gets about 60 phone calls a week from admirers and his fan mail numbers about 50 letters. He's a wow with everybody.'

Kenny Ball played Sunday 23rd August; the remaining three Sundays that month the sessions were provided by local bands.

The Kenny Ball Jazzmen played at the club Friday 18th September and the next evening on board the Royal Iris ferry for an end of season River Boat Shuffle, with MJB in support; the club was closed for that evening.

Saturday 26th September a first appearance for the Swinging Bluegenes much to the disgust of Harry Ormersher. Joan Aiello recalls Harry was not very pleased with this type of music.

Sunday 27th September The Jazz Committee with a line-up of Bert Courtley trumpet, Don Rendell tenor, Eddie Harvey piano, Pete Blannin bass, and Jackie Dougan drums.

Sunday 4th October the contrasting styles of the Bruce Turner Band and the Swinging Bluegenes. Fairweather-Brown All Stars and Kenny Ball completed this month's visiting bands. Sunday 1st November a return visit by The Jazz Committee.

The first week in November the club celebrated its first year with a Jazz Band Ball, the Kenny Ball Jazzmen playing Friday 6th, Saturday 7th, Sunday 8th.

Country music came to the club for the first time on Friday 20th with Johnny Goode and his Kinfolk with MJB, Clinton Ford, and Jill Martin.

Bruce Turner Jump Band

Visiting bands that month, Bruce Turner, Fairweather-Brown All Stars and from Bristol the Avon City Jazzband.

December and London bands playing included Diz Dizley (two gigs), The Jazz Committee, Kenny Ball (two gigs).

Thursday 24th December, Christmas Eve, Bags Watmough Band and Chris Hamilton Jazzmen.

Saturday 26th, Boxing Day, MJB, with Clinton Ford and Bags Watmough Band.

Thursday 31st December, New Year's Eve, MJB, with Clinton Ford plus Bags Watmough band bring in the New Year, the only night in the year that the local magistrates allow the bar to remain open after midnight.

1960

Clinton Ford singing to Jimmy Leech on his wedding night,
February 1960; others on stage Ray Ennis and Les Braid

Rose and Jimmy Leech wedding night, Mardi Gras, February 1960

Ralph 'Bags' Watmough speaking about the club's first twelve months stated: "the Mardi Gras was far superior to the Cavern, it was a much better set up and is a genuine night club". Frank Parr said: "the Mardi Gras was a very good jazz club, very civilised by the standards of the time".

Fairweather-Brown All Stars commenced the New Year Sunday session on 3rd January. The following Sunday 10th the Mick Mulligan Band with singer George Melly appears at the club for the first time. The band had been playing at the Cavern since its opening in 1957.

*Visiting bands for January, Wally Fawkes' Trogs,
Kenny Ball (two gigs) and The Jazz Committee.*

February the guest bands included Fairweather-Brown All Stars, Bruce Turner, and Mick Mulligan with George Melly. George commented his father much preferred it when we moved from the Cavern to the Mardi Gras as it was a much more commodious place – maybe the bar helped.

Wednesday 24th Rose Forman and Jimmy Leech get married and held the evening reception at the Mardi with entertainment provided by many local musicians including the Blue Genes and a young man on trumpet, 16 year old Alan Downey.

Sunday nights in March featured Fairweather-Brown, Kenny Ball, Bruce Turner and Mulligan and Melly.

That month also saw the departure of manager Harry Ormesher. He left to open a similar type of club, the Iron Door.

The April Sunday programme included Bruce Turner, Kenny Ball, Fairweather-Brown with Beryl Bryden, Mulligan and Melly.

A new addition to Stan and Jimmy's business with the opening of the Downbeat Club, Victoria Street in the city centre on Wednesday 27th April. The reason for opening this new club may have been due to Harry Ormesher opening the Iron Door Club on Saturday 9th April in nearby Temple Street, off Victoria Street, just a few hundred yards away. The Alan Alderson Quintet were the resident band; they had been playing at the Mardi in preparation for the opening of the Downbeat. The bar at the new club was open 12 noon to 6pm Monday to Saturday; this enabled it to take advantage of the rule that clubs allowed drinking after 3pm when public houses could only serve until 3pm, reopening again at 5:30pm.

Beryl Bryden

The Downbeat was a cellar venue and much smaller than the Mardi, with a capacity of 300. It opened in the evenings, Wednesday, Thursday, Saturday and Sunday. The hours of opening were similar to the Mardi, 7pm until 11pm with the bar closing at 10pm.

Most of the bands played at both venues. Members of both clubs were very loyal and would visit one or the other, eventually settling to stay at the club they preferred.

Fairweather-Brown started the Mardi month of May for visiting bands and the following Sunday playing at the club for the time, Ian Bell Jazzmen, later in the month Mulligan and Melly, and the Bruce Turner Band.

A number of changes this month: Jimmy was now secretary of both clubs, but on the advice of the police who suggested that it was not practical to manage both clubs he was to appoint another secretary for one.

Jimmy and Stan decided to appoint a secretary/manager for both clubs. Lennie McMillian was appointed to the look after the Downbeat.

I received a message from the manager of the MJB, Dick Goodwin – would I meet him at the Iron Door Club? They were playing there at a private function, after the club had closed. I went along about midnight (this was my first and last visit to this club), Saturday 14th May. Dick said Jimmy Ireland wanted a manager for the Mardi Gras to get in touch with him to arrange an interview.

I had a meeting with Jimmy at the Majorca Restaurant, Tarleton Street, the following Monday. Dick had recommended me to Jimmy; the interview didn't take too long, it was just a question of my duties, salary, and starting date. I had been unemployed for three months and glad of the opportunity of returning to full time employment, wages £10 per week, 'cash in hand', tax and national insurance paid. I started on Monday 23rd May. My duties included arranging bar, door, and cloakroom room staff, booking the bands and setting times they were required on stage, issuing membership forms and cards, and keeping a register of members. I knew most of the bands playing, having met them during my two years working at the Cavern. The London bands arranged with agent Jim Godbolt, which was subject to contract, and Jimmy preferred to sign himself.

The club opened at 7pm until 11pm, the bar closed at 10pm, the sessions started at 7:45 and finished 11pm prompt. Two bands played at the weekend, each band doing 2x 45 minutes spots. On Tuesday 'Jam' night, a resident trio would back any visiting musicians who wanted to play.

The snack bar had now changed, selling alcohol, but food was no longer available – it was considered that the grease from the food affected the draught beer, plus there being a bigger demand for beer. The two bars were managed by Jimmy Leech who lived in the flat on the premises with his wife Rose. Jimmy would prove to be the longest serving member of full time staff; other members of the staff included former professional boxer Alan 'Kid' Tanner and Stan's close friend Albert Lowe.

The first visiting band for June, Friday 3rd and
Saturday 4th Kenny Ball's Jazzmen,

At the end of the gig Kenny informed Jimmy Ireland that in future they would be playing at the Iron Door Club. This was quite a blow to the club after the two partners had helped to kickstart the band's career in 1958. Kenny felt that his allegiance was with Harry Ormesher who gave him a start, and to rub salt into the wound an advertisement in the Liverpool Echo the following week announced 'The Kenny Ball Jazzmen will in future be appearing monthly at the Iron Door club'. Kenny never worked again for Jimmy.

The visiting bands this month, Fairweather-Brown,
Ian Bell, Bruce Turner, Mulligan and Melly.

Sunday July 3rd Fairweather-Brown supported by the MJB, who had a new singer, Les Howard, making his Mardi debut. Les had been around a long time appearing with big bands, in particular the BBC Northern Dance Orchestra broadcasting quite often on the BBC Light Programme. Les borrowed an LP record of mine, 'Bob Scobey Frisco Jazz Band'; some of the numbers were part Clinton Ford's repertoire which the club members enjoyed. Les kindly returned my record, after many requests, two years later. Some of the Bob Scobey songs still remain part of the MJB programme today.

Sunday 10th July, Bruce Turner Jump Band with the MJB in support, quite a strong bill. John Chilton (trumpet) with the Turner Band commented: "I often come to Liverpool to play and it was always marvellous if the 'Mersey's' were on the same bill with us at the Mardi. I knew it was going to be a good evening and I could stand at the bar during my time off and hear some damn good jazz."

Sunday 24th Mick Mulligan and George Melly

Sunday 31st Ian Bell Jazzmen, plus MJB with Les Howard

Sunday 7th August Fairweather-Brown. Sandy Brown was very keen on his scotch whisky and complained that we didn't stock malt whisky, his favourites being Islay Mist and Laphroaig. Jimmy Leech duly corrected this omission, which made one Scottish clarinet player very happy, and both brands sold very well and became stock items.

Mick Mulligan Band with George Melly played the following Sunday – they were always a big draw at the club; appearing with them that night the Bluegenes.

Modern jazz, which was not readily accepted in Liverpool, appeared Sunday 28th August – the band that night Ross-Courtly Jazztet, all very talented musicians. The MJB completed the line-up that night.

Rose Leech, returning home one evening, was refused entry into the club by a new member of the door staff; the club was full even to members. Rose protested, "But I live here!" He replied, "I don't care if you sleep here, YOU CAN'T COME IN!" Another member of the door staff came to her aid, explaining to the new man that "Rose is the wife of Jimmy and lives here". The red faced doorman apologised – the man was only doing his job, but it caused a chuckle.

Stan and Jimmy would always try to improve the club, and not being too pleased with the height of the ceiling, about 40 feet, they decided it needed reducing. The cost of a 'false' ceiling was too expensive. With the collective thoughts of other members of staff, the answer, a net stretched across the club wall to wall would reduce the ceiling effect by 20 feet. The next problem: where would we find a supplier of a net 60x60 feet? After making enquiries locally it drew a blank. Who wants a net that size? Deep-sea trawler fishermen! We contacted a fishing net manufacturer in Fleetwood who supplied exactly what we needed. After battening the walls with 2x1 timbers, cup hooks screwed into the timber every 12 inches, came the hard part – stretching the net on to the hooks. After a couple of hours and a few expletives from Stan, job done, the net looked quite effective.

Another feature introduced was blue lights (ultraviolet). They had been installed at the Downbeat Club by a relation of Jimmy's and proved to be a great success. My father Henry, an electrician, installed five of these lights over the Mardi dance floor. They were an instant hit with the members. The lights made anything white stand out – shirts, dresses and false teeth. Some of the girls wore tight white dresses much to the delight of the lads.

The month of September and just two guest bands,
Ian Bell Jazzmen on the 18th and Bruce Turner
Jump Band on the following week, the 25th.

On Wednesday 28th the first of many American jazz presentations by Roberts and Ireland Ltd; mainly in association with London agent Harold Davidson. On this occasion the Miles Davis Quintet at the Liverpool Philharmonic Hall, tickets 6 shillings (30 pence) to £1. The line-up: Miles Davis trumpet, Sonny Stitt alto/tenor, Winton Kelly piano, Jimmy Co bass and Paul Chambers drums.

The Fairweather-Brown band kicked off the month of October on
the 2nd followed by Mulligan and Melly the following week.

Friday 14th and the return of Clinton Ford to sing with the MJB after
a successful summer season appearing at the Central Pier, Blackpool.

Sunday 16th the first visit by the Second City Jazzmen, Sunday
23rd Wally Fawkes' Trogs, Sunday 30th was advertised as a
'Great All Star Night' to celebrate the club's 2nd anniversary,
with Kathy Stobart (tenor sax), MJB with Clinton Ford,

The Alan Alderson Quintet featuring Lucille Renault.

November, visiting guest bands this month Mulligan and Melly, Fairweather-Brown, and Bruce Turner.

The month of December the following announcement appeared in the Liverpool Echo:

Management and Committee of

The only Mardi Gras Club

Mount Pleasant wish to

Announce

They are not Presenting

A Jazz Show on 16th December

At Any Other Place Than The

Only Mardi Gras Mount Pleasant

The Name Mardi Gras is

Registered Under the Registration Of Names Act.

Another organisation was using our good name to promote an event at St George's Hall. We had an idea who the promoters were but it was not worth the legal cost to prevent it happening.

Two new guest bands this month, Sunday 4th The Jazzmakers and Saturday 17th from Yorkshire, Mike Taylor Jazzmen. Bruce Turner Band and Fairweather-Brown completed the month for visiting bands. Saturday 24th, Christmas Eve, Bags Watmough Band plus Savoy Jazzmen. The club was closed on Christmas Day. Monday 26th, Boxing Night, Bags Watmough Band and Alan Alderson Quintet.

Saturday 31st The MJB with Clinton Ford plus Chris Hamilton's Jazzmen brought in the New Year.

Catering at Liverpool and Everton Football Clubs

When I joined Roberts and Ireland Ltd in 1960 they were the official caterers at Liverpool and Everton football clubs, another part of their business empire.

It was a perk of the job going to both grounds on match days. I had a pass allowing me in to any part at each ground. At Everton there was a special staff entrance in Gwladys Street. I would help serving teas etc in the Bullens Road stand, and watch most of the game. At Liverpool I entered the ground via the players and officials' entrance. I served in the snack bar just behind the Directors' box.

A testimonial match in 1961 at a packed Anfield ground witnessed the final game of the Liverpool legend Billy Liddell. It was a very emotional night. Bill, a one club man, was revered by all the supporters. After the game I went into the players' dressing room to present Billy with a huge meat pie with his name on top made of pastry. The pie had been made by our suppliers at their Aintree factory.

On match days at Anfield I'd wait in the corridor by the players' dressing rooms for Jimmy Ireland or Stan Roberts – they would be collecting the day's takings from all the catering kiosks. One occasion, standing in the corridor looking very lonely, I was approached by the Liverpool FC manager Bill Shankly, who enquired in his distinctive Scottish accent if he could help me. I explained my reason for being there and he seemed satisfied with my reply. I would then travel home with one of the partners before going on to my club duties.

A number of ladies who worked at both grounds also had jobs at the Mardi as bar and cloakroom staff, glass collectors and cleaners.

The following season the Littlewoods organisation became the caterers at both clubs.

Liverpool Press Club

I became an associate member of the club in 1961. The club catered for and was run by members of the national and local press. The club rooms were on the first floor of St George's Building, 24 to 32 St George's Place (Lime Street) in the city centre.

The club was allowed to serve members with alcoholic drinks until 1am due to a special exemption order; public houses were required to close at 10pm. Members gained entry to the club with their own key.

The club became part of our social life, after an evening working at the Mardi Gras. Friday was a popular night, often meeting showbiz personalities like Harry Secombe and Ken Dodd. Pantomime season you would meet cast members from the Royal Court and Empire Theatres. The club was strictly male only.

Most of the national daily papers had a local reporter; some had two, plus a photographer. Press members I recall included the Clare brothers Ron and Les, Bill Marshall, Frank Corless, Les Poole,

Freddie Aspden, Vic Slack, Durham 'TED' Paddock, Norman Dickson, Don Smith, photographers Stan Pope, Charlie Owens, Larry Sayle, Peter Ralph, and Walter McAvoy.

I met another member, Theo Kelly, former manager/secretary of Everton Football Club. Theo worked as a sales representative for the Littlewoods organisation. He made a note in his diary of all the hotels he stayed at giving his opinion, and his handwriting was perfect.

The club fruit machines were quite unusual in that they accepted the old brass 3d piece – they had been installed many years before gaming machines became legal.

It was quite common to be rubbing shoulders standing at the bar with the Lord Mayor of Liverpool still wearing his Chain of Office; he'd call into the club for a quiet drink after an official function.

Sunday night visiting jazz bands to the Mardi Gras looked forward to a relaxing drink and a game of snooker before setting off on their long journey home. One of the musicians, Pete Appleby, drummer with the Mick Mulligan Band, reckoned he could drive a car from Liverpool to London in less than four hours. The journey was mainly by 'A' roads with a limited amount of motorways. Jimmy Ireland said this was not possible and issued a £100 challenge which was taken up by Pete. A large crowd gathered in Lime Street outside the club to cheer Pete off at midnight. The London rendezvous being a public telephone box agreed by both parties, Jimmy was required to phone at 4am. When he did, Pete answered the phone, and won the bet. The next visit to Liverpool by the Mulligan Band, Jimmy paid up saying he'd received more than £100 worth of publicity about the incident within the music business.

Bill Marshall (Daily Mirror), the co-author of 'The Man Who Gave the Beatles Away', asked me for a lift home, but I don't think he appreciated my mode of transport, a Vespa scooter. I thought he lived on my route home to Aigburth, but he had moved into the home of the 'new' Mrs Marshall who lived six miles further on in Halebank.

Arriving about 1:30am he insisted that I meet his wife; the new bride woken and dragged from her bed to meet a complete stranger was not very pleased – she had a face like thunder.

With the pending demolition of the club building the committee had the task of finding a new home. Jimmy, by now a committee member, recommended the purchase of a large house within the Sefton Park perimeter, but this suggestion was rejected, and it was too far away from the city centre, instead settling for two floors above a showroom in Bold Street on the corner of Newington, with the entrance in Newington.

A member of the bar staff, Cecil, was well liked. If you were drinking he'd stay all night, quite often keeping the bar open until 4am, providing you were able give him a lift home to the other side of the Mersey.

A feature of the club's Christmas festive was the musical revue written and performed by the members. It was hilarious; Alan Williams, co-author of 'The Man Who Gave the Beatles Away' was a surprise performer singing like a soprano.

In 1968, now married with three young children, I couldn't afford to pay the annual membership fee of £10, so I sent a letter of resignation to the Club Secretary, Larry Sayle.

1961

Clinton Ford announced he would be leaving the MJB to join the Kenny Ball Jazzmen.

Clint had received a phone call from Kenny, who had seen him at the Mardi, and made him an offer to join the band. Jimmy Ireland advised him to accept the offer; he only stayed with the band a couple of months, leaving to go solo. Clint worked for the BBC Light Programme in his own series 'Clinton's Cakewalk' and appeared on TV in 'Stars and Garters', 'The Good Old Days' and 'The Billy Cotton Band Show'. He did work with the MJB when his commitments allowed.

Clint appeared with MJB on New Year's Day, with his 63rd and final performance on Friday 6th January. The Mick Mulligan Band and George Melly started the New Year for visiting bands followed by the Ronnie Ross-Bert Courtley Quintet on 15th, with Fairweather-Brown on the 29th.

The management presented at the Philharmonic Hall the Dave

Brubeck Quartet, also on the same bill the Joe Harriot Quintet on Thursday 26th, this promotion being in conjunction with Harold Davison Ltd; tickets 6 shillings (30pence) to 15 shillings (75pence) This concert was well attended.

The club's publicity, posters and newspaper advertisements were handled by an agent. I'd phone the agent with the details of who was appearing the following week, and they arranged poster sites around the city centre. I also delivered posters to Lewis record department, the Tatler News Theatre (we had the snack bar concession), Nems record stores in Great Charlotte Street and Whitechapel – each venue was given a free pass in to the club. It was at the Whitechapel store that I met Brian Epstein; he had a small office in the basement, and we would have a friendly conversation mainly about the music business. Little did I know that in a few years' time he would become the millionaire manager of The Beatles. Brian didn't show any interest during our conversation about live music or what was happening in Liverpool clubs, he never visited the Mardi and his only concern was for the Nems family business. When I heard that he had become manager of The Beatles I thought what does he know about the business?

Sunday 5th February a new visiting band, 'From London a promising new group Rod Mason with Lisa Spurr' – it was their only appearance.

Tuesday 7th February the return of a musician who had played trumpet with many jazz bands, now with his own band, the Les Harris Six. I also remember Les when he was member of the 2nd Allerton scout group in Mossley Hill; he played the bugle in the band.

Guest bands this month, Bruce Turner Jump Band, Mick Mulligan with George Melly, who always drew big crowds – George's theatrical style with songs like Frankie and Johnnie was well received – with the Fairweather-Brown All Stars appearing at the end of the month.

The ever popular Bruce Turner started the month of March for visiting bands; I enjoyed their mainstream arrangements, followed by Mick Mulligan with George Melly. Sunday 26th March the first visit of Dick Charlesworth and his City Gents with glamorous blues singer Jackie Lynn, the same singer who had appeared at the club in 1958 with the Bags Watmough Band. I missed this event having been injured playing football the day before; I was in hospital for four weeks with a further 15 weeks on crutches.

Sunday 2nd April the club debut for Trevor Kaye and his Trad Kings, Sunday 9th April Mick Mulligan and George Melly, Sunday 16th Bruce Turner Jump Band, Sunday 23rd Fairweather-Brown, Sunday 30th the second visit this month by Mick Mulligan and George Melly.

Monday 1st May Roberts and Ireland Ltd present The Giants of Jazz, Thelonious Monk Quartet, stars of the Jazz film 'Jazz on a Summer's Day', also Art Blakey's Jazz Messengers, the group that has sold more records in the USA than any other modern jazz group, at the Philharmonic Hall, tickets 6 shillings (30p) - £1.00.

The Fairweather-Brown All Stars started the month of May Sunday 7th; the band's second visit in two weeks, Sunday 14th Bruce Turner Jump Band, Sunday 21st the new sensational London group Kenny Barton's Oriole Jazz Band, also MJB with Jill Martin. With the absence of Clinton Ford, Jill, who had joined the band from the Dark Town Skiffle Group, was now the main vocalist, with contributions from banjo player Ken 'Nob' Baldwin and clarinet player Don Lydiatt. Sunday 28th return visit by Trevor Kaye and his Trad Kings.

Sunday 4th June first time on Merseyside the White Eagle Jazz Band. Sunday 11th a return by popular demand of Kenny Barton's Oriole Jazz Band, Sunday 18th Mick Mulligan and George Melly, Sunday 25th Bruce Turner Jump Band.

Sunday 2nd July Fairweather-Brown All Stars, their first visit for two months, Sunday 9th Bruce Turner Jump Band.

Saturday 15th Roberts and Ireland Ltd present Chris Barber's Jazz Band with Ottilie Paterson at the Philharmonic Hall, tickets 4/-,5/- and 6 shillings (30pence). Chris enjoyed his motor sport and this gig was arranged for the same day as the 'Aintree 200'. This event took place on a motor racing circuit within the Aintree Racecourse, home of the world famous Grand National. The financial arrangement for this gig: the band received 60% of the ticket sales, Stan and Jimmy 40%; they also paid all the expenses leaving them with a small profit.

Sunday 16th Mick Mulligan and George Melly, Sunday 23rd Britain's new sensation The Original Downtown Syncopators.

Sunday 30th two local bands, possibly to cut costs, this being the main holiday period when factories closed and there is a two week general exodus from the city.

Sunday 6th August the Ed Corrie Concord Jazzmen.

I returned to my club duties after an absence of 19 weeks – during this period I received just £5 per week, so I was glad to be back working.

Sunday 13th Bruce Turner Jump Band, Sunday 20th Mick Mulligan and George Melly, Sunday 29th great return of Kenny Barton's Oriole Jazz Band.

Sunday 3rd September Fairweather-Brown All Stars, Sunday 10th Bruce Turner, Sunday 17th another first, London's newest sensation The Gerry Brown Jazzmen.

Sunday 24th Mick Mulligan and George Melly.

Jimmy Tarbuck was a regular club member; he was working on the next block up Mount Pleasant as a sales assistant in an electrical retail shop. He was an old friend from my days as a boy scout in Mossley Hill. I often gave him a lift part the way home. He was just starting to appear as a comedian in the local social clubs. A Sunday night about 7:30pm Jimmy came into the Mardi panicking. He had a gig in Earlestown about 20 miles away and without transport, he wanted to borrow my car. I refused this request explaining my insurance was third party and covered myself only. I don't know if he ever made it on time.

Sunday 1st October Bruce Turner Jump Band, Sunday 8th Fairweather-Brown All Stars, Sunday 15th return visit by

*the Original Downtown Syncopators, Sunday 22nd and
for the second time this month, Bruce Turner Jump Band,
Sunday 29th Kenny Barton's Oriole Jazz Band.*

The club's 3rd anniversary passed without any celebration. The attendance at the club was now increasing week by week to the point that on some nights the 'House Full' sign went up. It was definitely the 'in place' with queues forming early in the evening with the management refusing admittance to visitors within an hour of the doors opening to allow space for members, and later in the evening even members would fail to gain entry.

*Sunday 5th November Bruce Turner Jump Band, Sunday 12th
Mick Mulligan and George Melly, Sunday 19th Fairweather-
Brown All Stars, Sunday 26th Kenny Barton Oriole Jazz Band.*

Thursday 23rd at the Philharmonic Hall, Dave Brubeck Quartet, tickets 7/6 to 15/- (75 pence), this concert was a complete sell-out.

Sunday 3rd December first visit by the Back O'Town Syncopators.

*Sunday 10th a double first, two London bands on the same
night, Fairweather-Brown All Stars and Wally Fawkes' Trogs.
Wally was the creator of the Daily Mail strip cartoon 'Flook',
George Melly contributed to the script and would often be typing
in the Mardi band-room catching up with the storyline.*

*Sunday 17th Bruce Turner Jump Band plus the Les Harris
Six, Sunday 24th, Christmas Eve, MJB with Jill Martin*

plus Chris Hamilton's Jazzmen. Tuesday 26th, Boxing night, Dave Lind Jazz Band, Savoy Jazzmen with Julie Kaye, plus Jam Session. Sunday 31st MJB with Jill Martin and Dave Lind Jazz band bring in the New Year.

Private Parties

Private hire of the club was an important part of the business. The club could be hired on Monday, Wednesday and Thursday when the club was closed. We averaged 60 bookings a year, December being particularly busy. One year during December I had just one night off and that was Christmas Night; the club was booked solid from the end of November. For £40 you got two bands or groups, a bar extension until 11:30pm and as a treat draught beer was sold in pint glasses. It was a condition that you couldn't sell tickets to members on the club premises and no public advertising.

One organisation, The Automatic Telephone Co (The Auto), Edge Lane, apprentices booked the club four times a year and they were always a sell-out. By way of a change the social secretary Mal Reader requested an outside group called The Beatles. I'd heard about this group from the Bluegenes and the noise they produced from their 100 watt speakers. I persuaded Mal to use one of our club groups to which he agreed and that's how close The Beatles came to playing at the Mardi! Mal lived in Coral Avenue just around the corner from where my future wife Jean lived in Kingsway, Roby. Mal later emigrated to Canada; I often wonder if he remembers how close he came to booking The Beatles or that I blocked them from appearing at the club.

The Inland Revenue hired the club for a staff union general meeting. The thought behind it being to attract the younger members to the meeting followed by dancing, but this wasn't repeated.

The club didn't have a licence for private parties; it was my duty to find a licensee who would attend the magistrate court to obtain an 'occasional licence' to enable us to sell alcohol. The club was supposed to clear the bar of all drinks and the licensee restock with his own supply, but this never happened nor did the licensee ever attend, one of the conditions for an occasional licence. If the police called, which they never did, I had to say he's just slipped back to his pub due to a problem. The licensee from Ma Boyles in Old Hall Street and the Albany Restaurant I can recall helping us with this problem. The Licensing Act eventually altered enabling me to obtain a 'Club Justice-On' licence. This allowed the club to sell drinks to members and visitors, with private functions restricted to ticket holders, tickets to be sold in advance of the event, no cash to be taken on the night of admittance.

Obtaining this licence meant that it was necessary for me to become a director of Roberts and Ireland Ltd.

1962

Sunday 7th January the last visiting band of 1961 became the first of the New Year, Bruce Turner Jump Band. Sunday 14th a second visit by Ed Corries Concord Jazz Band, Sunday 21st first visit by Jerry Brown's Jazzmen, Sunday 28th Fairweather/Brown All Stars.

Sunday 4th February Ian Bell's London Jazzmen, Sunday 11th Bruce Turner Jump Band, Sunday 18th Kenny Barton's Oriole Jazz Band, Sunday 25th the best from Bonnie Scotland with the first visit of Forrie Cairns the Clansmen featuring Fionna Duncan. Sunday 4th March Mick Mulligan and George Melly, their first visit for three months, Sunday 11th Dick Chalesworth and his City Gents featuring Jackie Lynn, Sunday 18th Fat John's London Jazzmen, Sunday 25th Fairweather-Brown All Stars

Sunday 8th April Roberts and Ireland Ltd, in association with Norman Granz and Harold Davison, present Count Basie and his Orchestra, with the sensational vocal group Lambert, Hendricks and Ross. At the Empire Theatre 5:40pm and 8pm.

*Sunday 1st April, MJB with Jill Martin and Bags Watmough
Band, Sunday 8th Bruce Turner Jump Band, Sunday 15th
Dick Charlesworth with Jackie Lynn, Sunday 22nd*

*Mick Mulligan and George Melly, Sunday 29th first
visit by JimMcHarg's Scottsville Jazzband.*

Wednesday 2nd May another Roberts and Ireland presentation
at the Philharmonic Hall, Louis Armstrong All Stars, with Gerry
Brown's Jazzmen, at 6:15 and 8:30pm tickets 7/6d (37½p) to £1.
We were all of the opinion Louis would be a big enough attraction
to fill two performances. The 6.15 performance had 200 paying
customers, Jimmy giving away 100 tickets to club members to help
boost the attendance. The 8:30 performances had an audience of
1200; one performance would have been the better option, making
it a sell-out. I was able to meet Louis again showing the band the
photograph taken six years earlier at the Liverpool boxing stadium,
Trummy Young being particularly interested as it featured him. The
entire band signed the photograph which I still treasure.

A young Bill Kenwright visited the club with his dad who was a
good friend of Jimmy Ireland. Bill had just made a record and had an
early copy (an acetate) with him. I introduced and played the record
on the very poor club sound system. I can't remember the name of
the record and I don't know if it ever went on general sale; I'll be
kind and say no more.

*Sunday 6th May Fairweather-Brown All Stars, Sunday 13th
Bruce Turner Jump Band, Sunday 20th Kenny Barton's Oriole*

Jazz Band, Sunday 27th Mick Mulligan and George Melly.

Wednesday 30th Roberts and Ireland Ltd present the World's greatest pianist, first appearance in this country of Errol Garner, who wrote 'Misty', at the Philharmonic Hall at 8pm. Tickets 7/6d (37½p) to £1. This concert was a sell-out. Jimmy took Jimmy Tarbuck, who had recently made his debut at the London Palladium, and introduced him to Errol in the Green Room.

Errol Garner

The club was now losing business turning members away having reached capacity on most nights; the only way we could increase the club capacity was up with another floor. An architect was appointed to prepare a feasibility study to find extra space. A balcony was the answer. Plans were prepared and presented to the local council planning department.

Sunday 3rd June Fat John's London Jazzband, Sunday 10th Bruce Turner Jump Band featuring the new Scottish Singing Sensation Jeannie Lamb who became a club favourite.

Friday 8th a new venture, Roberts and Ireland Ltd present a Whitsun jazz festival featuring Mr Acker Bilk and his Paramount Jazzband, also Bruce Turner Band and Merseysippi Jazz Band at the Tower Ballroom New Brighton 8pm to 1am, late transport arranged, tickets 7/6d (37½p)

Tuesday 12th the advertisement for the club in the Liverpool Echo stated for the first time, 'STRICTLEY MEMBERS ONLY VISITORS NOT ADMITTED', which was not correct. The message we were trying to imply was, if you're not a member you can't just enter the club, but you can accompany a member as their bonafide guest.

This advice had been given by a senior police officer. We anticipated the notice may affect attendances, but it had the reverse effect: people were more determined to become members with the result of the club being busier than ever.

Sunday 10th June Bruce Turner Jump Band with Jeannie Lamb, Sunday 17th Kenny Barton's Oriole Jazzband, Sunday 24th a band new to the club, Mike Shores' Tuxedo Jazz Band.

Sunday 1st July Gerry Brown's Jazzmen, Sunday 8th Jim McHarg Scottsville Jazzband, Sunday 15th Fairweather-Brown All Stars, Saturday 21st annual visit to Liverpool for the Aintree

200 by Chris Barber's Jazzband featuring Ottile Paterson with an evening concert at the Philharmonic Hall, tickets 4 shillings (20 pence) and 7/6d (37½p). Sunday 29th, two local bands possibly saving money due to the annual local holidays.

Sunday 5th August Fairweather-Brown All Stars, Sunday 12th Forrie Carins and the Clansmen, featuring Fionna Duncan, Sunday 19th Kenny Barton's Oriole Jazzband – on the same day a promotion by the well-known jazz impresario George Webb, a riverboat shuffle 'The Merseysippi Jazz Boat', on board an Isle of Man ferry. The trip to the Island and back started at 10:30am from the Pier Head, and on board were Mr Acker Bilk's Paramount Jazzband, Kenny Ball's Jazzmen, Terry Lightfoot's Jazzmen, Monty Sunshine's Jazzband, Bruce Turner Jump Band, The Saints Jazzband, plus five other top trad jazzbands. Tickets £2 and you could pay by instalments. Jimmy and I were guests of George. The boat arrived back in Liverpool at 10pm, and all the bands moved on to the Mardi for a 'night-cap'. One member of Acker's band fell asleep and was locked in the club all night; he was released in the morning with the arrival of the cleaners.

Sunday 26th a quick return visit to the club by Bruce Turner's Jump Band. Tuesday 28th, this week's programme is being run in association with Merseyside Arts Festival.

Sunday 2nd September Fairweather-Brown All Stars, Sunday 9th Bruce Turner Jump Band, Sunday 16th Gerry Brown's Jazzmen, Sunday 23rd Ed Corrie's Concord Jazzmen, Sunday 30th Dick Charlesworth and his City Gents featuring Jackie Lynn.

Jean and I visited the Blue Angel Club after work at the Mardi on a Friday night. Sitting on large settees in the ground floor bar area another couple sat opposite, we shared a table to place our drinks. I didn't have a clue about the other couple until Ringo Starr walked in. I recognized Ringo from my days at the Cavern. He started talking to the other couple, mainly about the successful night they had had. I then realised that the couple opposite was John Lennon and his new bride Cynthia.

The Blue Angel was always packed from midnight with groups and people who worked in the club business, no doubt all talking 'shop'.

The beginning of October The Beatles released their first record 'Love Me Do'; it meant nothing to us at the Mardi, our only music interest being jazz. The Swinging Blue Jeans were the top group in Liverpool and it was only a matter of time before they would be competing for the top spot.

The construction of a balcony started in October, increasing the capacity of the club by 200/300. During this period when the club was open it was necessary to have an 'army' of cleaners to dust down and make the place presentable.

Sunday 7th October Bruce Turner Jump Band, Sunday 14th Forrie Cairns and the Clansmen, Sunday 21st Fairweather-Brown All Stars, Sunday 28th after an absence of four months Mick Mulligan and George Melly.

The Balcony was now at the half way stage of completion, the biggest task being the main steel girder which stretched from wall to wall. This was quite a feat of engineering. A crane parked at the back of the building in Chapel Lane lifted the girder into position; it was then guided through a hole made into the club wall and placed into its final position. The girder rested on two steel supporting posts which were already in place, the position of these posts being six feet inside the dance floor. The main bar alongside the emergency exit had to be reduced by half to accommodate the new stairway to the balcony. It was necessary to remove most of the lighting and make safe the electrical wiring and remove bar furniture. This work was carried out by members of staff on a Sunday night after the club closed at 11pm. The building contractor would be installing the new staircase the next day.

Sunday 4th November and a quick return from Scotland by Forrie Cairns and the Clansmen with Fionna Duncan, Sunday 11th Gerry Brown's Jazzmen, Sunday 18th Bruce Turner's Jump Band.

Friday 22nd November John F Kennedy, the American President, is shot. This news was flashed on TV at 6.45pm just as I was leaving home for the club. I arrived at the club at 7pm and went straight into the office to watch the unfolding news on TV from the US: Kennedy was dead.

Sunday 25th November Mick Mulligan and George Melly.

The Balcony was now near completion, with a staircase on either side of the club. The one on the right as you walked into the club went straight up, on the opposite side it had been necessary to reduce the size of the bar by half to make way for the staircase which ascended in two stages. The bar at the back of the club had now been removed, tables and chairs were now placed in this area with large mirrors on the walls which gave the effect of the club looking bigger.

Cy Tucker with Earl Preston's TTs releases 'My Prayer' on the Fontana label.

Sunday 2nd December Sandy Brown All Starts (no Al Fairweather), Sunday 9th Dick Charlesworth and his City Gents with Jackie Lynn.

Balcony bar

The 2nd week in December the Balcony opened, the estimated capacity being 200 but often that figure was more like 300 plus.

Sunday 16th Mick Mulligan and George Melly, Sunday 23rd Bruce Turner Jump Band, Monday 24th, Christmas Eve, MJB, with Jill Martin, also Swinging Blue Jeans. The club was packed, but with the MJB on stage at about 9pm there was a power failure. The place was plunged into complete darkness which didn't affect the band — they just carried on playing. Plan 'B', the emergency lighting came on and a supply of candles placed around the club. The candles were in stock from the last power failure in November 1958. The main fuse board was situated in Turner's Auction Room below the club. A quick decision to break into the Auction Room as an emergency was considered necessary. I jumped in my car to go home to Aigburth and fetch my father Henry, an electrician. I had phoned to let him know about the problem so that he could gather his tools etc. We returned to the club in about 25 minutes to find that the electricity had been restored. In less than 30 minutes repairs had been completed with the help of a club member who was an electrician, and normal service was restored just in time for the Blue Genes to go on stage. Jimmy rewarded the electrician with free entrance to the club for life. Dad's reward, a couple of pints with thanks from Jimmy and Stan.

The next day, Christmas Day, Jimmy instructed me to call at the Auction Room to check that everything was secure, but it was too late: the Proprietor Eddie Duffy had already been and secured the rooms with new locks. Stand by for trouble! After my visit to the premises I arranged to pick up Rose and Jimmy Leech, and with Jean we planned to visit the Unicorn pub in Cronton, this being a rare night off for Jimmy and myself. Driving towards Cronton I ran out of petrol in Tarbock Road near St John's Road, Huyton. Just where do you get petrol at 8pm on Christmas Night? I wasn't

MARDI GRAS CLUB, LIVERPOOL

a member of the AA or the RAC. Eventually after two hours of searching for petrol, the owner of a petrol station who had earlier refused to help me out relented after I pleaded for help and I gave him £5 for a gallon of petrol, the cost of a gallon at that time being 12 shillings (60p). Returning to the car with my passengers frozen with the cold we returned to Jean's home in Kingsway for hot cups of tea. Not the best way to spend Christmas night. Sunday 30th Sandy Brown plus Al Fairweather with the All Stars. Monday 31st MJB, with Jill Martin plus Blue Genes brought in the New Year.

The Escorts

The Escorts made their debut at the club Friday 20th September 1963. They appeared on seven occasions until Friday 8th November, but for some reason didn't appear again until Tuesday 14th January 1964. With the success of the Swinging Blue Jeans they were signed up by Jimmy Ireland and became regulars at the club. The group's line up, Mike Gregory bass guitar, Pete Clark drums, Terry Sylvester guitar/vocals, John Kinrade lead guitar. All the members of the group being under 21 years of age, their parents were required to sign the contract. I had the task of visiting their homes on behalf of Jimmy to have the contracts signed. All the boys lived in the South Liverpool area. Terry lived in Hurstlyn Road close to Forthlin Road, home of Paul McCartney.

Photographs were important for fans and publicity. The more unusual the photograph the better chance you had of it being in the press. I had to take the group for a photo shoot and chose the gardens of the bombed out church, St Luke's in the city centre. After a few photographs around the gardens I spotted a wooden ladder belonging to a maintenance worker propped against the church wall.

The worker allowed me to borrow the ladder to enable the boys to climb onto a ledge just inside the wall; this was on the Bold Place side of the church. The group standing looking over the castle type wall, the photographer – I think his name was Gordon Whiting – took his shots from ground level, and yes they were different. The group were all minors; I was responsible for their welfare. With today's health and safety rules I shudder at the thought of the risk I took making the group do such a dangerous task. I contacted Terry via email asking if he had a copy of the photograph – not only did he not have a copy he couldn't remember the event.

The Escorts outside the Mardi Gras. (L to R) Mike Gregory, Pete Clark, John Kinrade and Terry Sylvester

Terry and Mike eventually joined the Swinging Blue Jeans, and some years later Terry joined The Hollies. He now lives in Florida, a very wealthy man; he was inducted into the New York Rock n' Roll Hall of Fame March 2010.

The group made 96 appearances at the club, the last being Tuesday 13th June 1967.

1963

The first week of the New Year a solicitor's letter arrived on behalf of Mr Duffy complaining about the break-in. The partners apologised for the action they had taken and promised it would never happen again. It was also agreed with Mr Duffy that the main fuse board be moved into the club, and also a three phase supply was installed to cope with the increase of electricity. Peace restored, we were always good neighbours and that is how it remained for many years.

During the renovations to the cloakroom area an old fire grate being removed revealed a small linen bag which contained three King George Third one penny coins and a small piece of paper – in a circle the size of a five pence piece was an inscription which was invisible to the naked eye. I sought the help of a Press Club member named Des, a reporter with the Liverpool Daily Post. I visited Des at his office in Victoria Street and under a powerful magnifying glass he solved the mystery, the inscription on the piece of paper being the Lord's Prayer, the linen bag would have been placed there when the Chapel was built in 1790. This was without doubt the living accommodation for the resident Minister and his family. A report written by Des of this find appeared in the Daily Post. The coins were damaged and of no value and were eventually thrown away.

An announcement in the Liverpool Echo, Sunday 20th January 5:40pm and 8pm at the Empire Theatre, Duke Ellington and his Famous Orchestra, tickets 5/- (25 pence) to £1. This promotion was in association with Harold Davison and Norman Granz.

Sunday 6th January Forrie Cairns and the Clansmen with Fionna Duncan, the last visit by this fine Scottish band. Sunday 13th Mike Cotton's Jazzmen.

A week before the Ellington concert a Special announcement in the Liverpool Echo, Roberts and Ireland Ltd regret that due to reschedule of programme there will only one performance of the concert at 8pm. This was due to poor ticket sales for the early performance, possibly a shortage of money after Christmas.

Sunday 20th Mick Mulligan and George Melly, Sunday 27th Fat John's London Jazz Band.

Jimmy and Stan, looking for more space, hit on the idea of building an office above the band room which was a single storey. The band room was relocated next to the stage. The full size snooker table was demolished and thrown away – we had tried to give it away but there were no takers. The entrance to the new office, which was very palatial, was via the balcony. Planning permission for the new office had not been obtained and it was not long before City Council officials, seeing the start of the construction, stepped in, halting the work until planning was granted. Plans were quickly prepared by the architect who had designed the balcony. Plans were approved after a short period and the work continued. The former band room now became the ladies' cloakroom with plenty of space and mirrors. During the winter the girls would dress according to the weather; travelling by public transport was the only afforded able way into the city centre. They would be dressed with a heavy top coat, scarf, hat, cardigan, gloves, and winter boots, and carry an umbrella so they would need plenty of space to change ready for the dance floor. The girls who didn't deposit their handbags in the cloakroom would place them on the dance floor and dance around them. The boys were more straightforward – they would have a Mac or an overcoat and some wouldn't bother with either.

Saturday 2nd February making their first appearance The Dauphin Street Six, Sunday 3rd Fairweather-Brown, Sunday 10th Gerry Brown's Jazzmen, Sunday 17th one of the country's most popular bands, the Alex Welsh Band, making their first appearance at the club, another band no longer required by the Cavern Club, Sunday 24th Bruce Turner Jump Band.

Sunday 3rd March Roberts and Ireland ltd present Ella Fitzgerald and the Oscar Peterson Trio at the Empire Theatre 5:40pm and 8pm. Ella was very popular and seemed to make an annual visit to Liverpool. Before the concert I asked Ella to sign an LP cover of one of her albums. There was debate about the photograph on the cover and how old she was when it had been taken. Both performances were well attended.

Sunday 3rd March Ed Corrie's Concord Jazz Band, Sunday 10th Sandy Brown's All Stars (no Al Fairweather) – Sandy was voted Britain's number one jazz clarinet player in the Melody Maker polls. Sunday 24th Fat John's London Jazz Band, Sunday 31st The Humphrey Lyttleton Band making their first appearance at the club. Humph, as he was known, was one of the biggest names in the Jazz business. Most of the 'name' London bands were now appearing at the club, the Cavern changing over to mainly beat groups and dropping jazz on most nights.

Sunday 7th April Gerry Brown's Jazzmen, Tuesday 9th with a new name, the Bluegenes, now managed by Jim Ireland, change their name to the Swinging Blue Jeans. Sunday 14th Fat John's London Jazz Band. Sunday 21st debut for one of Scotland's best known bands, Clyde Valley Stompers. Sunday 28th Fairweather-Brown All Stars with the brilliant Tony Coe.

Sunday 5th May Mike Cotton's Jazzmen. Sunday 12th Bruce Turner Jump Band, Sunday 19th a quick return for Fairweather-Brown with Tony Coe, Saturday 25th Jill Martin makes her last appearance at club with the MJB to be replaced by Pam Peters. Sunday 26th Dick Charlesworth and his City Gents with Jackie Lynn.

Jimmy Ireland appointed London agent Jim Godbolt to be sole agent for the Swinging Blue Jeans and John Chilton as the group's PR man. Both men were well known to Jimmy, Jim Godbolt being an agent for quite a number of London jazz bands and John Chilton played trumpet for many years with the Bruce Turner Band. John commented: "Jim Ireland was my great pal and there was period when he often had a jazz group on with a skiffle or beat group. The beat groups played opposite the jazz attractions at the Mardi and you could sense that something was going to change. Soon the beat groups were the main attraction."

Swinging Blue Jeans with PR man John Chilton

In June 1963 the Swinging Blue Jeans released a record on the Parlaphone label, 'It's Too Late Now'. Jim Godbolt came up with the idea of 'buying' the record into the music charts. He had obtained a list of record shops who supplied information to the trade for them to compile a list of the best-selling records for that week and this is how the record 'Charts' were organised. Jimmy Ireland agreed with this arrangement.

My fiancée Jean Davies, being a shorthand typist, agreed to take notes of the list of the shops. Godbolt phoned the club on a

Saturday night at 11:30pm; Jean took notes until 1:30am including a short toilet break. During this period I stocked two bars, Jimmy Leech being on holiday. Jean typed the list of 100 record shops. The following Monday morning Lennie McMillian set off with £200 to buy as many records from the shops on the list.

The operation proved to be a success when the record reached the top 50. The group was not aware of this arrangement. Jim Godbolt quoted in his book *All This and Many a Dog* that the group's fee increased from £30 per night to £75.

Sunday 2nd June, Gerry Brown's Jazzmen. Sunday 9th Bruce Turner Jump Band.

Sunday 16th a visit by a band from Sweden, that country's top jazz band Anders Hasslers Cave Stompers. Sunday 23rd Dick Charlesworth and his City Gents featuring Jackie Lynn.

Tuesday 18th June Rosalie (Rose) Leech received an invitation to Paul McCartney's 21st birthday party being held at the home of a relative in Dinas Lane, Huyton. During the evening Rose had an altercation with John Lennon. It's alleged that Rose hit Lennon across the face; Lennon reacting punched Rose in the stomach. The Cavern DJ Bob Wooler came to the aid of Rose, remonstrating with Lennon; Bob in return received a beating from Lennon. The story of this incident was told to me the next day by Rose and was soon rife amongst the Liverpool club scene. Bob Wooler kept quiet about the incident, most people believing that he was 'paid-off' by Lennon. Perry Leech, the son of Rose and Jimmy, confirms that his mother told him about this incident with Lennon.

Spencer Leigh, writing in his book 'The Best of Fellas' tells the story of Bob Wooler, in a chapter 'Punch Drunk', devoting seven pages to this incident. Sadly Rose died in January 1984.

Sunday 30th Fairweather-Brown All Stars with Tony Coe.

Johnny Sandon and the Remo Four

Friday 5th July first time at the club for Johnny Sandon and the Remo Four playing alongside the MJB with Pam Peters. Sunday 7th July Mike Cotton Jazzmen.

Sunday 14th Mulligan and Melly. Sunday 21st Fairweather-Brown All Stars with Tony Coe. Tuesday 23rd Swinging Blue Jeans plus

Johnny Sandon and the Remo Four, the first night at the club without a jazz band. Sunday 28ᵗʰ Bruce Turner Jump Band.

Sunday 4ᵗʰ August Fairweather-Brown All Stars with Tony Coe. Sunday 11ᵗʰ August Bruce Turner Jump Band. Sunday 18th Dick Charlesworth and the City Gents featuring Jackie Lynn. Sunday 25ᵗʰ Mike Cotton Jazzmen.

COUNT BASIE
AND HIS ORCHESTRA

Count Basie

Sunday 1st September Fat John's London Jazz Band. Sunday 8th a new pattern emerged. Sunday had always been jazz bands only, featuring guest bands from London supported mainly by local bands, MJB, Chris Hamilton's Jazzmen, Bags Watmough; these bands would also play at the club during the week. On this particular Sunday the MJB with Pam Peters played alongside the Swinging Blue Jeans. They had appeared together on many occasions, but this was the first time for a beat group to play on a Sunday.

Tuesday 10th Roberts and Ireland Ltd in association with Harold Davison present the World Famous Count Basie Orchestra with Jimmy Rushing plus Sarah Vaughan with Kirk Stuart Trio at the Odeon (cinema) London Road 6:35pm and 8:40pm tickets 10/- (50p) to £1-1s (£1:05p). This concert was well attended. After the show all the artists were invited to the club for drinks, which most accepted including 'The Count'. I had a long conversation with the Basie drummer Sonny Payne who told me about his love of horses.

Playing at the club that night were Johnny Sandon and the Remo Four, and making their debut Earl Preston's TTs. Local and national newspaper photographers were present and took photographs of Count Basie on stage with the Earl Preston group. One national newspaper had a photograph with the caption 'Basie Meets Mersey Beat'.

Sunday15th Gerry Brown's Jazzmen. Sunday 22nd Humphrey Lyttleton Band, the second and last visit by this band.

Sunday 29th Bruce Turner Jump Band, on the same night the Swinging Blue Jeans appearing alongside their PR man John Chilton. The Blue Jeans on this night commenced a pre-recorded 13 week series on Radio Luxemburg sponsored by Lybro Jeans.

The 'Blue Jeans' story is one of growing success . . .
(watch the charts!) T.V. dates, nationwide tours
recording sessions . . .
AND NOW those chart-storming Merseysiders
are featured every Sunday at 9 p.m. in
LYBRO's Luxembourg Show "SWINGTIME"

Comment from the group:
"With a name like ours we
naturally go in for jeans in a
big way – and that means
LYBRO JEANS.
LYBRO JEANS are really
SWINGING! Especially the
new shade – named after us
"SWINGING BLUE".
That is why, everywhere we
go, we go LYBRO!

Go LYBRO!" LYBRO in 'Swinging Blue'

LYBRO'S
new hit
shade

Sunday 6th October MJB with Pam Peters, Sunday 13th Alex Welsh Band, Tuesday 15th debut for Sonny Webb and the Cascades, Sunday 20th Fairweather-Brown All Stars with Tony Coe, Sunday 27th Mike Cotton Jazzmen. The club's 5th anniversary passed without any celebration.

*Friday 1ˢᵗ November Roberts and Ireland present in association
with Harold Davison, Errol Garner, who wrote Misty, he was
described as the World's greatest pianist, at the Philharmonic
Hall, tickets 7/6 (37½ pence) -£1. This concert was a sell-out.*

*Sunday 3ʳᵈ November Bruce Turner Jump Band. Tuesday night was
now taken over entirely by beat groups. Sunday 10ᵗʰ Mick Mulligan
and George Melly, Sunday 17ᵗʰ first visit by Alan Elsdon's Jazz Band,
Sunday 24ᵗʰ Dick Charlesworth and his City Gents with Jackie Lynn.*

Sunday 1ˢᵗ December Bruce Turner Jump Band with Swinging Blue
Jeans who were about to release their next record, *Hippy Hippy
Shake.* Jimmy Ireland had given me a preview of this record a couple
of weeks earlier and I commented that it would be a hit. Friday 6ᵗʰ
debut for the Connoisseurs who included singer Vince Earl, who
later became a stand-up comedian and maybe better known as Ron
Dixon in the TV Channel 4 soap opera *Brookside.* Saturday 7ᵗʰ
The Beatles appear on BBC TV Jukebox Jury, one of the records
discussed being *Hippy Hippy Shake.* John Lennon commenting
it would be a small hit, they sound better since getting rid of the
banjo player (Paul Moss), George Harrison stating "I think it could
possibly be a hit – I know for a fact it's a popular song around here;
we used to do it ourselves". All four Beatles voted the record a hit.

*Sunday 15ᵗʰ Fairweather-Brown All Stars, Sunday 22ⁿᵈ Mike
Cotton Jazzmen also appearing and making their club debut
former Beatles drummer Pete Best and the Original All Stars.
Tuesday 24ᵗʰ, Christmas Eve, another group making their
first appearance, Karl Terry and the Cruisers. Thursday 26ᵗʰ,*

Boxing Night, Swinging Blue Jeans; they had also appeared that evening in Z Cars on BBC TV. Sunday 29th Bruce Turner Jump Band. Tuesday 31st, New Year's Eve, the MJB brings the New Year in with Earl Preston's TTs and The Young Ones.

I had become very friendly with the Empire Theatre manager Neil Brooks due to my involvement organising jazz concerts. During the pantomime season Neil was very busy and not able to attend football matches at Liverpool Football Club where he had two tickets for the Directors' Box. He invited me to use one of the tickets, the agreement being I called at the theatre, gave his wife a lift to the game, and returned her later to the theatre. This happened twice and it was most enjoyable: a reserved place in the club car park, tea (in a china cup) and biscuits at half-time, at full time back into the Directors' Room for something a bit stronger. The room was a bit of a disappointment – it was like a canteen, but as an Evertonian I was nevertheless grateful for Liverpool's hospitality. Another perk knowing Neil we were able to obtain tickets for shows at the theatre without any hassle. As part of our friendship we gave Neil's son a free pass to the Mardi which he used quite often. Neil in his showbusiness career had been manager of the famous Lancashire comedian Frank Randel; he later progressed to become general manager of the London Palladium.

1964

The club continues to draw big crowds each week with the addition of the balcony being a great success. It was what you would call Liverpool's 'in-place'; the demand for membership continued to grow weekly. The management being very strict, the club was trouble free, which was appreciated by the members who commented "we feel safe".

The Swinging Blue Jeans are high in the record charts make an appearance on BBC TV in a brand new programme *Top of the Pops*. The position of the record is not clear: some charts have them at No1 others say No2. The group were in competition with The Beatles' *I Want to Hold your Hand* and the Dave Clark Five's *Glad All Over*; the three records had sold more than four million copies in total.

In a book written by Spencer Leigh, *The Best of Fellas*, about Cavern DJ Bob Wooler, Bob stated, "In the summer of '63, following a lunchtime session at the Cavern, I got a call from Brian Linford, manager of the Mardi Gras club, who asked if he could borrow Chan Romero's '*Hippy Hippy Shake*' and return it within the hour, which he did. I thought he wanted the song for the Escorts who were under the Mardi's management. It never occurred to me that he wanted it for the Blue Jeans because they had upright bass and banjo then. The Blue Jeans were jumping on the bandwagon – a classic case of 'If you can't beat them, join them.'" This statement wasn't true, just another of Bob's fibs, I had nothing to do with this arrangement. Sue Johnston, the girlfriend of Blue Jeans drummer Norman Kulke, who was working for Nems Record store, brought the record to the Mardi for Jimmy Ireland to pass on to the group; Sue is now a well-known and much loved actor.

Sunday 5ᵗʰ January no visiting band on this night, MJB with The Kubas, Sunday 12ᵗʰ Alan Elsdon's Jazzband , Sunday 19ᵗʰ Mike Cotton Jazzmen, only two visiting bands this month, Sunday 26ᵗʰ MJB with Pam Peters.

Friday 24ᵗʰ Roberts and Ireland Ltd present Frank Sinatra Junior, Tommy Dorsey Orchestra directed by Sam Donahue, with Jeannie Thomas and Larry O'Brian, and also Helen Forrest, Charlie Shavers and The Pied Pipers, at the Odeon Theatre, London Road, 6:35pm and 8:40pm, tickets 7/6d (37½p) to 17/6d (87½p). During the first house performance the house lights went up. I was standing at the back of the auditorium with the theatre manager and I asked for an explanation as to why the lights had been switched on, but he couldn't give a reason. We both hurried back stage. With Helen Forrest on stage it was at her request that the house lights came up – she would only sing if she could see the audience.

I didn't meet Frank Sinatra Junior and reports that he appeared at the Mardi Gras are not true. This concert was not a success.

With more beat groups playing at the club some of the less popular jazz bands were now being dropped. In the month of February with just one visiting band on the 9th, Fairweather-Brown All Stars – this was their last engagement at the club – an excellent band of professional musicians as were all the other visiting bands. This was to be the beginning of the end for the jazz era. The MJB with Pam Peters appeared on the remaining three Sundays.

During this month the Rank Organisation filmed the Swinging Blue Jeans for their *That's Life Series*. I was given the job of organising the outside locations, all filmed in one day. The first location was in Sefton Park with Ray Ennis walking his dog. He was then surrounded by a posse of admiring female fans (recruited from members of the club) demanding his autograph. The next scene took place outside the Empire Theatre in Lime Street, which I had arranged with my friend Neil Brooks, the theatre manager; the group were seen running into the theatre giving the impression that they were about to appear in a concert. The third and final outside location was filmed at Cranes Music Shop in Hanover Street. The shop was one of my club poster sites, and the group were shown handling guitars before buying. The final scene was filmed inside the Mardi on a Thursday night before an invited audience of club members. The place was packed with a fantastic atmosphere. The Blue Jeans played for about an hour with the film crew stopping and starting to get the best shoots and positions. The filming and release were timed to coincide with the group's next single, *Good Golly Miss Molly*. Another group also played that night continuing the entertainment after the completion of filming. The music scene was moving fast in Liverpool mainly due to the enormous success of The Beatles; agents were arriving by the coach load signing many local groups. Jimmy Ireland also joined in the stampede signing The Escorts, Earl Preston's Realms and Cy Tucker. With these three groups, they were all under 21 years and so for each individual member their mother or father was required to sign the agreement on their behalf. I had the task of calling to their homes to have the contract signed.

On behalf of
THE RANK ORGANISATION
I wish to extend to you a cordial
invitation to attend a special press
screening of the new 'Look at Life' entitled
'SOUND OF A CITY'
featuring — The Swinging Blue Jeans
at 10.30 a.m. on Thursday March 19th
at the GAUMONT, LIVERPOOL
G. W. Cranfield.
Manager.

5th March the first Friday night without a jazz band, groups featured that night were Denny Sayton and the Sabers and The Secrets.

The Escorts release their record on the Fontana label *Dizzy Miss Lizzy/ All I Want Is You.*

The Blue Jeans film had a private viewing at the Trocadero cinema, Camden Street in the city centre. The Dave Clark Five who were appearing in the area attended a special showing as guests of Jimmy Ireland. I received a letter from the producer Harold Shampan thanking me for all my work in making the film a success.

The MJB and the Bags Watmough Band continued to play regular sessions during the month of March. Tuesday 17th, St Patrick's night, the debut of Earl Preston's Realms.

A record crowd attended that night with more than 1100 people; maybe the fact that members were admitted free helped. 29th March the first Sunday without a jazz band, it was Easter Sunday, the groups that night, The Escorts and Cy Tucker's group.

Monday 30th Jean and I were married at St Aloysius RC Church Huyton-with-Roby; a former altar boy at this church was Ray Ennis.

Jimmy now constantly occupied his plush office. He had a secretary, Gaynor Schofield, and his nephew Derek Dolman helped to run the Blue Jeans fan club. The media would refer to Jimmy as owner of the club, but with the publicity he was receiving Stan did not feel too pleased and a rift started to upset the partnership. They had recently opened a gourmet restaurant The Albany, Old Hall Street in the city centre. The initial advertisement described it as the *most expensive restaurant in Liverpool*, not the best way to attract custom. It had cost many thousands of pounds to convert this old watering hole which had been frequented mainly by cotton brokers. This venture in my opinion was a costly mistake.

EARL PRESTON and The Realms

Representation : Jim Godbolt Agency Ltd
145 Wardour Street London, W.1
Regent 8321-2

Management : Jim Ireland
Mardi-Gras, Mount Pleasant, Liverpool 3
Royal 4448

Earl Preston and The Realms

The MJB and Bags continued to provide the jazz element during April. Wednesday 22nd Roberts and Ireland Ltd in association with Harold Davison present the Modern Jazz Quartet, with John Lewis (piano), Milt Jackson (vibraharp), Percy Heath (bass), Connie Kay (drums); Guest artist Laurindo Almeida, guitar. At the Philharmonic Hall Wednesday 22nd April at 8pm. Tickets 7/6d (37½p) - £1:00.

Friday 1st May Roberts and Ireland Ltd in association with Harold Davison present the American Folk Blues and Gospel Caravan with Sonny Terry and Brownie McGhee, Muddy Waters, Sister Rosetta Tharpe, also Mississippi John Hurt, Rev; Gary Davis, Cousin Joe Pleasant and Otis Spann, at the Philharmonic Hall at 8pm. Tickets 6/- (30p) to 20/- (£1). The *Liverpool Echo* made a mistake with the advertisement in the Thursday 30th April edition stating that the concert commenced at **3pm.** I made a complaint about the error and the *Echo* agreed to place an advertisement in the Friday edition twice the size of the original free of charge giving the correct time. I also insisted on, to which they agreed, sending a photographer to the Lord Nelson hotel where the artistes were staying to take a photograph. Muddy Waters was most helpful but could only 'round-up' two other members, Rev Gary Davis and Cousin Joe Pleasant. The photograph appeared in the Friday edition of the newspaper stating the concert was an evening performance. The concert was a complete sell-out. After the show all the artists were invited to the Mardi for drinks. With Jimmy Ireland away on business his wife Jessie allowed the bars to stay open until 2am, free drinks for all present. Photographer Barry Farrell took the opportunity of taking a photograph of the artists and local musicians including Tony Davies (The Spinners), Ray Ennis, Ralph Ellis (Swinging Blue Jeans) and

Earl Preston's Realms who were appearing at the club that night and provided the backing for the 'jam session' later. The whole evening was brilliant from start to finish. Muddy Waters was the inspiration behind the naming of the Rolling Stones.

Jam Session at the Mardi, seated (L) Tony Davies (The Spinners), (R) Ray Ennis (Swinging Blue Jeans). On stage Muddy Waters with other cast members plus Earl Preston and The Realms

Saturday 2nd May debut for Cy Tucker's Friars. A competition was held to name the new group with Friars being the winning entry. Tucker, as he was known, had played with Earl Preston's TTs previously. He had a distinctive voice; when he met Paul McCartney in the Blue Angel Club Paul congratulated him for his version of the Timi Yuro song *Hurt*.

Tuesday 5th Billy Kinsley's group The Kinsleys make their debut.
Billy was a talented musician and deserved a lot more success;
Jimmy Ireland recognised his talent and later signed him up.
Sunday 10th Bags Watmough Band reforms as Bags Blue Beats.

The Swinging Blue Jeans commence a nationwide tour with Chuck Berry, also on the same bill the Rolling Stones. Within a week the Blue Jeans had to abandon the tour due to the hostile audience reception – their type of music was not acceptable. A tour of Germany was hastily arranged by Jim Godbolt. There was a problem: Ralph Ellis and Les Braid were not in possession of their passports. I called at Les's home to collect his, but there was nobody at home in Ralph's. A phone call was made to the headmaster at the school that Ralph's brother attended in Halewood, I went to the school to collect the boy, take him home, get the passport and return him back to school, job done!

Sunday 17th the Chuck Berry concert at the Liverpool Empire. Jimmy Ireland instructed me to call at the Empire to welcome the Rolling Stones to Liverpool and invite them to the Mardi for drinks. Gaynor Schofield came with me, she being a RS fan. Due to my friendship with the theatre manager Neil Brooks I had no problem gaining entry to the dressing room. I introduced myself to the Rolling Stones and shook hands with all members of the band and invited them to the Mardi for drinks. They didn't accept our hospitality, which was a pity, because they missed Cy Tucker's Friars and Bags Blue Beats.

Jimmy Ireland presenting Swinging Blue Jeans with Silver Disc for Hippy Hippy Shake at the Mardi Gras

Tuesday 26th a rare appearance by the Swinging Blue Jeans on their return from Germany. It was normally free to members on Tuesday but on this occasion the admission charge was 5/- (25 pence). The boys were glad to be back at their 'home' and were overwhelmed by the reception. It being the 22nd birthday of Ray Ennis, I presented him with a bottle of champagne with Jimmy Ireland presenting the group with a Silver Disc for a quarter million sales of *Hippy Hippy Shake.*

The MJB were now the only jazz band appearing at the club, and it was now becoming difficult to present jazz and beat on the same night. The beat fans would stay silent and not dance when jazz was being played. The jazz fans resented beat music and also the younger age group it attracted. A decision was made to drop jazz altogether after six and half years, so on Sunday 7th June the MJB played their last regular gig after a period of five years. Derek Vaux had just joined the band on bass due to the retirement from playing by Dick Goodwin. It was a sad occasion for me, having known the band for 11 years, to tell them that the club could no longer offer them any more work.

I'm pleased to say that myself and the band remained friends for many years.

The jazz bands had a very loyal following, they had spending power over the bar that would be missed. A lot of friends I'd known for many years following jazz disappeared. An incident I'll always remember about Dick Goodwin, having a quiet drink at the end of the evening, Jimmy Leech decided to have a go at playing Dick's string double bass. When he finished he stood the bass against a wall at the side of the stage; as he walked away there was almighty clatter – the bass had fallen off the stage and broken the neck; it was now in two pieces. Dick reacted as it were a family bereavement, he was stunned. Dick played the instrument left-handed; he couldn't get a replacement and had to wait for a repair before playing again.

A search for new club premises was a priority. Searching the local press property page and visiting estate agents became a weekly task. The premises had to be in the city centre, at ground or first floor level, at least 3000 square feet and a clear span, without posts or any other obstructions. I discovered the ideal premises on the corner of Seel Street and Slater Street. The owner of the property enquired as to the nature of my business. I always kept the reason for use quiet, not stating it was for entertainment and a licensed club – we were frightened of another promoter jumping in and snatching a good site from under our nose. On this occasion I told the property owner it was wanted for a licensed club. He then revealed to me that he had intended to open it for similar use and in fact had registered the premises with local authorities as the Mirabel Club. I reported back to the partners this gem of a find, fitting all the requirements for a successful city centre club. I'll write more about this club later.

The club's magnificent grand piano was now hardly used; the only person playing it was Bags Watmough with his Blue Beats. After 10 gigs they played for the last time on Saturday 29th August. The piano was now surplus to requirements. Frank Robinson, pianist with the MJB when playing at the club for the first time, commented, "It was a nice big grand piano with a lovely tone instead of the little upright at the Cavern."

The piano was well looked after and maintained. A piano tuner from Rushworth and Draper, who was blind, would call every Thursday. We met him at the club entrance and guided him up the stairs and onto the stage. With his work completed he'd have a glass of pale ale before moving on to the next job.

With the overwhelming success of The Beatles and all the other Liverpool groups the city became a Mecca for journalists to leave the comfort of London, travel north and write about the exploding music scene in Liverpool. Most of them concentrated on the Cavern, but the Mardi also had its share of the phenomenon. Foreign TV crews came to film the attraction of the Mersey Beat. The writer and TV personality Daniel Farson called, accompanied by Cilla Black acting as his guide around the club scene.

The Swinging Blue Jeans agent, Jim Godbolt, in his book *All This and Many a Dog* stated: "These shattering changes were to alter the pattern of many agents' activities, mine included. Jazz clubs, and the bands that relied on them for best part of their income, folded. At the height of the trad boom there were forty bands on the road. The numbers quickly dwindled to a mere half dozen."

The club was now packed every night, new members from Wigan, Warrington, Widnes, St Helens and Southport, all from outside the Liverpool area. A young lady reporter from a Lancashire evening newspaper had an assignment enquiring about the increasing popularity of the club. I explained that the club was free of trouble and having a licensed bar didn't create any problems. The members realised that any bad behaviour and they would be barred, so it did not happen.

The article in the newspaper was quite big, complimentary and in a prominent position with the headline, 'Beat Club Daddio says Beer is Best'. I was a Daddio at the age of 28.

The partners were always looking to further their business empire mainly by way of new clubs. A club in Birmingham was put up for sale and Jim Godbolt enquired if we would be interested. Jimmy sent me to Birmingham to have a look at this cellar type Cavern club in the city centre. I met up with Jim Godbolt in a hotel where we stayed overnight. In the evening we met the owners of the club to give it our assessment. A cellar club was not on our agenda, preferring carpets and a decent wooden dance floor. The club, in my opinion, had very little potential.

We called the next morning to inform the owners of our decision that we wouldn't be recommending any further interest. As we entered the much darkened club Jim fell into a manhole, the cover having been removed by a maintenance worker. The hole was full of water, and for the next hour Jim sat in the office drying his shoes and socks. Could this have been preconceived anticipating our decision!

We departed at Birmingham railway station, Jim going to Grimsby for a weekend jazz festival and myself to Liverpool. I reported my findings to the partners; there was no further interest in this club.

The future format of two groups per night became the standard. We had the choice of more than 400 groups on Merseyside. Most of them played basic music in the charts at the time, but the more professional groups set their own style and programme with a mixture of beat, country or R&B. Tuesday night we held auditions

117

– the majority were not sufficiently experienced and with a limited repertoire, but it gave the groups something to aim for. Some of the more talented musicians were picked up by other groups. When I compiled the weekly programme the first names to go in the diary were the groups managed by Jimmy: The Escorts, Cy Tucker's Friars, Earl Preston's Realms and The Kinsleys; in the event of a more profitable gig for one of the groups they could be 'pulled-out' and replaced by another group; they were assured of regular work each week.

Former Liverpool City Councillor and Deputy Labour Leader Derek Hatton was a regular member at the club on Tuesdays and Fridays. When interviewed on local radio he commented that when attending the Mardi Gras the same groups like the Escorts would be performing, not that he was complaining about the standard of entertainment. Many years later I explained to Derek the policy of booking Jimmy's groups first, and he said how much he enjoyed the club.

Some of the other groups with regular bookings were The Asteroids, The Kirbys, Gerry De Ville and the City Kings, The Coins. The Hideaways make their club debut Friday 18th September.

On the 22nd September a new musical, Maggie May, written by Lionel Bart and Liverpool scriptwriter Alun Owen opened at the Adelphi Theatre, London. Maggie May was a mythical Liverpool prostitute. The club scene in the show was based on the Mardi. Alun and stage designer Sean Kenny visited the club several times to get inspiration and the club atmosphere. The musical had a pre-opening at the Palace Theatre, Manchester; Liverpool would have been the ideal place but unfortunately the Empire Theatre was not big enough for such a big production. The people involved with helping in the production were invited to the opening night in Manchester – Jimmy, Stan, Jimmy Leech, Lennie McMillian, and me.

We were met in the Theatre foyer by Alun who introduced us all to Lionel Bart who thanked everyone for their help and co-operation.

After the show the cast and invited guests returned to Liverpool for a party at the Blue Angel Club; this was hosted by club owner Alan Williams. One of the guests present was Judy Garland. I had met Alun Owen previous to this – his dad Sid lived in Lyttleton Road, Aigburth, the next road to where I lived. Alun was also the screenwriter of the Beatles' debut feature film *A Hard Day's Night*. A member of the cast was a Mardi member Geoffrey Hughes, later to become Eddie Yeats in Coronation Street; Geoffrey would help out occasionally when the club had staff shortages.

Friday 2nd October first appearance at the club for The Hillsiders.

Rory Storm, being a keen footballer, was manager and captain of the Merseybeat football eleven, playing matches on a Sunday for charity. Rory approached me for a match against a Mardi team which I accepted. Before the game could be played I had to register the team with the Liverpool County FA and pay a fee. The Mardi paid for the match programmes which I delivered to Rory's home in Broadgreen Road. The game took place at the Co-op sports ground Fazakerley on Sunday 18th October.

The Merseybeat team were a bit of a surprise and won the game 3-2, one of their outstanding players being Eddie Parry from the Dennisons. Jimmy Ireland insisted that he played (he was an Everton shareholder) but I substituted him at half-time – after all, he was in his forties. This was the only game played by the Mardi team.

The relationship between the partners was becoming more strained; news about this must have leaked, with the local and national media making frequent enquires about a possible breakup of the partnership. Norman Dickson of the Daily Herald being the most persistent reporter – he took a great interest in the Liverpool music scene.

Some changes occurred during November affecting two of the groups. The Escorts' drummer Pete Clark left; he wasn't happy with the type of music being played by the group. He was replaced by Kenny Goodlas, a member of the Kirbys for four years.

Earl Preston's Realms split amicably with manager Jimmy Ireland. They made their 38th and what was thought to be their last appearance at the club on Saturday 7th November. This announcement came as quite a surprise with the group being very popular and having a big following at the club.

December and another busy month for private bookings. I worked every night except Christmas night, such was the popularity of the club; social organisers knew they wouldn't have a problem selling tickets for their event. Cy Tucker's Friars were very popular and got most of the work, Cy's repertoire of party melodies like the Hokey-

Cokey and Knees up Mother Brown were well received during the Christmas party season. Cy was one of the busiest musicians in Liverpool; he refused to turn professional, preferring instead the security of his full time job as a postman.

Thursday 24th December, Christmas Eve, three groups appeared: The Kirbys, Cy Tucker's Friars and The Stereos. Cy Tucker would do a double, also appearing at the Downbeat Club.

Saturday 26th December, Boxing Night, Swinging Blue Jeans, The Kinsleys and The Asteroids. There was talk among the staff about the possibility that the proprietors were about to dissolve their partnership. This was the final club appearance of the Swinging Blue Jeans even though they called the club their home.

Jean Linford in conversation with bar staff

Thursday 31st December, New Year's Eve, The Kinsleys, The Dions and The Secrets see in the New Year; another packed house, the doors being closed before 9pm.

1965

The Partners decided that it was time to dissolve the partnership. I don't know if the split was due to a disagreement over the running of the many business aspects within the company or personal fallout. I got on well with Jimmy and his family, wife Jessie, children Stephen, Valerie and Vivien, as well as Stan and his wife Ann, children James, Robert and Jayne.

The American concerts had ceased and although the club was still busy and the top attraction in Liverpool, little progress was being made. The groups were in Jimmy's sole control; since the initial success of the Blue Jeans' *Hippy Hippy Shake* and a top 20 follow up with *Good Golly Miss Molly* not a lot was happening with them or the other groups in his stable. Jimmy was considered by many to be the 'brains' of the organisation, with Stan the grafter looking after maintenance and any odd jobs.

They both worked at the club on alternate nights and only occasionally together on busy nights or special occasions.

Jimmy's (always referred to as J I) personality and business acumen was never in doubt. His home was 6 Fulwood Park, Aigburth, previously the home of Mrs Blackler of the famous Liverpool city centre department store Blackler's. The large mansion, which featured in newspaper articles and TV programmes, was in about two acres of ground with stables and a lodge for a gardener/handyman. Jimmy was a tall and handsome man with a pencil moustache with a fine physique who kept himself fit. He had a fine business brain and would be comfortable in any company. He was originally from what was notoriously known as 'under the bridge' in the south Liverpool district of Garston where he was well known. At the end of his working life he went to live in America near his son Stephen in California before returning to the UK.

Stan Roberts you would class as one of the boys. He wasn't like a boss, not very tall, and bald. I don't think his upbringing was as smooth as JI; he worked mainly in the building trade as a labourer. His wife Ann had won a considerable amount of money on the football pools but it was not something we talked about. When I met him he lived in Copper Avenue, Mossley Hill before moving on to Aughton and then onto Blundellsands before settling in retirement in Tenerife. I have found it difficult to contact any members of Stan's family.

Jimmy's relatives working within the business included Jessie's brothers Donny and Jack Lyle, nephews Donny Lyle and Derek Dolman; Stan's son James worked in the Fruit Machine department.

Jimmy, during business hours, was very keen and didn't tolerate any mistakes, socially he was very affable and generous, and often after work at the club we'd go to the Blue Angel, Cabin, or Press Club for a drink. Stan was one of the boys who mixed and worked with most of the staff but rarely socialised after work.

The Fruit Machine business was taken over by one of the mechanics, Harry Owen.

Rory Storm and the Hurricanes made their one and only appearance Tuesday 2nd February.

In March Jimmy Ireland placed an advertisement in the *Mersey Beat* newspaper stating the address of his new office 56/58 Seel Street. He had acquired the premises of the Mirabel Club, and it also said it was the address of the Swinging Blue Jeans and The Escorts fan club. Cy Tucker's Friars and The Escorts continued to play at the club.

Jimmy Leech received a notice from Stan with a request for his family to move out of the living accommodation, with their two boys James and Perry. Rose was pregnant with her third child. It was considered to be overcrowded and not the best environment to bring up three children, a club in the city centre. There was also the thought that the club needed the extra space.

New groups making regular appearances included Denny Seyton and the Sabers, The Riot Squad, The Secrets, The Pretenders, The Pathfinders, The Feelgoods, The Stereos, and The Delmonts.

The club being in a hotel area we occasionally had social visits from an artist appearing in the city. Jimmy Leech kept a VIP visitors' book, and among the celebrities who signed the book were Dionne Warwick, and a vocal group The Raindrops, one of their members being Vince Hill. Peter Bonetti and Peter Osgood of Chelsea FC were staying at the Adelphi Hotel when they paid a visit. The club was popular with some of the Everton and Liverpool Players, Ian Callaghan being a regular member.

In May Jimmy and Rose bought a three bedroom terraced house in Wingate Road, Aigburth. The house became a 'Mecca' for some noisy parties. Most people invited were in the entertainment business and wouldn't arrive until after midnight. The Kenny Ball band, although no longer playing at the Mardi, remained good friends of Rose and Jimmy and were frequent visitors when in the area. I'm sure that neighbours living in close proximity would remember these frequently held events.

Friday 2nd July Earl Preston's Realms make a surprise return visit.

One rainy night a dishevelled looking character stood inside the doorway sheltering from the rain, he was waiting for a bus to take him home to Huyton. The young man noticed that The Delmonts were appearing that night, so he told the doorman the group were friends and could he say hello to them. He was allowed in, and within 10 minutes he was on the stage singing with group. The singer's name was Freddie Starr.

Freddie continued to sing with The Delmonts for the next couple of weeks. The leader of the group approached me about an increase in the fee because Freddie would be continuing as their lead singer. I agreed to an increasing their fee from £8 to £10. Freddie and The Delmonts became a big attraction and it was not long before Freddie started his comedy routine. It's the only occasion I can remember the club members stopping dancing and crowding around the stage, to watch Freddie's performance. A friend of Stan's, Bob Woodward, was the manager of the Cabaret Club, Duke Street. Bob came to the club to see Freddie's performance and immediately gave Freddie and the group a week's work at the Cabaret Club. After their week in cabaret they didn't appear at the Mardi again, preferring instead the club cabaret circuit. Stan was pleased with this arrangement due to the fact that when Freddie was on stage nobody drank, which affected the bar takings. Freddie, after his appearance on Hughie Green's Opportunity Knocks, became a national star as a comedian.

Freddie Starr

Sunday 29th August the first appearance by the Clayton Squares.

In October I received an offer from Jimmy Ireland to become manager of the soon to open Beachcomber Club. I would be working six nights a week until 2am. After a discussion with my wife Jean I decided not to accept the offer, while thanking Jimmy for his consideration. The manager's job was then offered to the Downbeat Club manager Lennie McMillan, who accepted.

Sunday 17th October The Big Three make their first appearance at the club. They had been playing for quite some time, mainly at the Cavern.

Friday 22nd October, Freddie Starr and The Delmonts, their final club appearance before they embarked on a nationwide tour.

Tuesday 9th November the 44th and final appearance by Earl Preston's Realms.

Sunday 14th December The Fix makes their club debut. They were different from the usual groups, they had the normal line up, drums, bass guitar, rhythm and lead guitar but in addition they had trombone, trumpet alto sax and singer Steve Aldo.

1966

The first week in the New Year an announcement in the *Liverpool Echo:*

Jim Ireland (Enterprises) Ltd present The Beachcomber Club to open Wednesday 12ᵗʰ January. Most exotic club on Merseyside.

Your host Len McMillan. Membership personal application only.

The jazz scene in Liverpool was now neglected so it was decided to have an occasional Jazz Night on Thursdays featuring top London bands. The first of these nights was held on Thursday 20ᵗʰ January with, for the first time at the club, the Chris Barber Jazz Band featuring Pat Halcox and Ian Wheeler. Tickets 6/- (30 pence).

The night proved to be successful with a sell-out crowd.

The Mardi was no longer involved with the American jazz concerts but Jimmy Ireland continued to present the concert himself.

February and the Cavern Club closes due to financial difficulties.

In a book 'The Best of Cellars: The Story of the Cavern Club' by Phil Thompson, a Cavern member, Yvonne Harris said: "In 1966 it closed its doors. I remember going into a zombie-like state, wondering where we would go, how we would see our favourite bands, but what we didn't realise was that we were growing up and sooner or later we'd have left the old Cavern anyway. It opened up a few doors down some time later, but it wasn't 'our Cavern' then, it wasn't special any more. By that time we'd found another club we loved, the Mardi Gras, but that's another story." I recall the author of this book, Phil Thompson, phoning me at home a few years earlier and holding a conversation which lasted about two hours. He wanted information about the Cavern Club and my memories during the two year period that I worked there. When his book was published he didn't acknowledge me though, despite me giving him two hours of my time.

Other venues around Merseyside were closing due to lack of support. The Mardi Gras was going from strength to strength and was now considered to be the biggest and financially the most successful venue in Liverpool. The impeccable behaviour of the club members being the key factor. Members were still commenting that they felt safe and comfortable in a very friendly environment.

Thursday 3rd March and our 2nd 'Jazz at the Mardi Gras' featuring Terry Lightfoot's Jazz Band, Tickets 5/- (25 pence), not a sell-out but it was well attended and gave the management encouragement to continue with these jazz evenings.

Thursday 17th, St Patrick's night, Kenny Ball's Jazzmen. This was the first appearance at the club by the band since they defected to the Iron Door Club. The band made their first appearance at the Mardi when they were completely unknown, and since that time they had become international stars with many records in the pop charts, such was the interest in traditional jazz at that time. The tickets at 6/6d (32½p) sold very quickly and the evening was a sell-out. The bonus for the club being the bar takings, an older crowd and good drinkers; it was nice to see old faces back at the Mardi. Thursday 31st another jazz night with Bob Wallis Storyville Jazzmen, tickets 5/-d. (25p), not a sell-out but well attended.

Thursday 7th April Terry Lightfoot's Jazz Band tickets 5/-d, (25p) another good night of jazz.

Thursday 14th a quick return visit by Kenny Ball, tickets 6/6d, (32½p) another packed night and excellent bar takings.

The number of groups appearing at the club was growing including Mark Peters and the Method, The Notions, The Dimensions and The Dresdens. Friday 15th debut for The Dennisons, their drummer Clive Hornby later played Jack Sugden in the ITV soap opera Emmerdale.

Thursday 28th Monty Sunshine Jazz Band, tickets 5/-d. (25p), well attended.

Thursday 12th May return visit by Chris Barber's Jazz Band featuring guest artist Kenneth Washington.

Tickets 6/6d (32½p) and another sell-out night.

Saturday 14th Cup-Final day at Wembley, Everton v Sheffield Wednesday, I was lucky to get a ticket. After the game, coming out of the stadium I bumped into Jimmy Ireland and Lenny McMillan and travelled back to Liverpool in the comfort of Jimmy's Mercedes, ending the evening celebrating Everton's win at the Beachcomber Club.

Thursday 16th June Mr Acker Bilk and his Paramount Jazz Band supported on the night by the Merseysippi Jazz Band. It was nice to welcome the MJB back to the club. Tickets priced at 7/6d (37½p) and another packed house. This was the one and only club appearance of the Acker Bilk Band.

The organiser of the football World Cup hospitality in Liverpool encouraged entertainment establishments to provide and be ready for an influx of football fans to the City. The Brazilian team would be based in Liverpool, playing their three qualifying games at Goodison Park, the home of Everton Football Club. The Brazil team were favourites to win the competition. Most of the city centre clubs took up the invitation; the Mardi decided to open every night from Tuesday 12th July to Sunday 31st. The local magistrates granted a bar extension each night until 2am with dancing until 2:30am, the exception being Saturday when the bar closed at 11.30pm – bar extensions were not allowed to continue into Sunday. A number of clubs applied for extensions until 4am which were granted. The Mardi programme covered most age groups. The Kenny Ball Jazz band played for four nights at the enormous cost of £500. Pianist

Dougie Evans, office manager at the Cavern, played with his trio on a couple of nights. The rest of the programme was made up of local groups. The expected thousands of visitors to the City did not materialise, it was a big flop, not just for the Mardi but for most of the City. The Brazilian supporters were billeted in London in preparation for the final to be held at Wembley Stadium. They travelled by train to Liverpool and returned after each game, and Brazil failed to reach the knock-out stages of the competition.

Tuesday 23rd August the first appearance for The Seftons, a very young group who had a big following. This created a problem: we were now attracting a younger age group. The club now had a Justices 'On' Club Licence which allowed police in plain clothes to visit the premises at any time, exam the visitors' book and the list of members. I held the licence on behalf of the club and because of this I was made a director of R&I (Entertainments) Ltd. The police visits, which were frequent, were made by an Inspector and a Constable. During the next couple of years I became very friendly with the officers; their tour of duty lasted about six months. Some of the officers would call into the club for a social drink, and on one occasion 10 officers were standing at the bar; it was just like a police club. There were no complaints from the police about the age of members or any infringement of the licensing laws, and we had an excellent relationship. One of the constables, Albert Kirby, later became a Detective Superintendent, when he retired becoming a crime consultant for ITN News. Another police officer who called at the club was Detective Constable John Evans who in later years was knighted when he became the Chief Constable of Devon and Cornwall Constabulary; I played football against John when he played for the Liverpool Police team. Constable Neil Ablett (father of Gary) is another member of the Liverpool Police team I played against; he was always in the company of Inspector Aled Parry. One Inspector, who was known as 'Otto', after his tour of plain clothes duty would call every December just to wish everybody a Happy Christmas. Otto attended court on one occasion to oppose one of my applications for a bar extension. The reason I gave was that Garston Swimming Club water polo team were playing in the final of a cup competition, some of our members played for the water polo team and wanted to celebrate, or drown their sorrows after the game. The magistrates granted the extension. Otto, after the hearing said, "I was just doing my job", or maybe he was thinking of Christmas. Some police officers were not successful in their careers. An inspector who was the least friendly of all insisted that the club visitors' book should include the visitor's address; I disagreed with his suggestion and continued with just the name of the visitor. This officer who was called 'a high flyer' later served a term of imprisonment. A sergeant who at one period called as a plain clothes constable was also sent to jail for a number of years.

The Beachcomber Club was becoming very popular with a lot of the older Mardi members; they were now drifting towards Jimmy Ireland's new club. They had Len McMillan as manager and Alan Tanner working as a doorman. This club also had a gaming room, a restaurant and a 2am liquor licence.

We were approached by a local artist to do something called kinematic art. Not managing to convince us on his first visit, he set about explaining the project in more detail. Screens would be erected around the walls of the club on two sides and over the stage. The screens of white canvas on large wooden frames were not flat but curved, or rather wavy. In the centre of the club, over the dance floor, a kaleidoscope of various coloured pieces of glass suspended from the ceiling rotated slowly, driven by an electric motor. Two powerful spotlights would shine on the glass producing fantastic coloured shapes which changed every few seconds on to the screens. The cost of this, £600, was paid by Ind Coup, the suppliers of Double Diamond, on condition that we sold only their products. Whitbread's, our suppliers at that time, refused to contribute towards the cost and were replaced by Ind Coup. The work on this project took three weeks to complete. I can't recall the name of the artist whose work was unique.

The bar at the Mardi continued to close at 10pm, with the occasional bar extension. To obtain an extension you had to write to the magistrates, explaining your reason for the extension of permitted hours. I was required to attend the court, usually on a Thursday morning, to answer any questions the bench may ask – it had to be for a special occasion. One of my applications was to celebrate the 16th birthday of Prince Charles, and when asked by the Chairman of the bench, "do you always celebrate his birthday", I replied "no, your Worship, but we will do so in the future". The application was granted. The granting of a bar extension was not always guaranteed. I was paid an extra £2.00 for each extension so it was worth my while to come up with a good 'excuse'. A number of clubs in the city centre now had a 'Super' licence, serving liquor with food until 11:30pm, or a special hour's certificate, usually those with a restaurant serving until 2am. The Mardi didn't have the facilities, a kitchen etc to comply with the required hygiene standards. Food was never served during my time as the club manager.

The age group attending was now dropping considerably to the point where we were now concerned about young people under the age of 18. A decision was made to ask all new members to produce their birth certificates; their date of birth was then included on their membership card. We considered this would satisfy the licensing authorities and police that we were operating the club to comply within the law. To a point this operation was a success, but eventually it backfired. New members in the 20 plus age group objected to being asked for their birth certificate and these potential members drifted away to clubs like the Beachcomber, which had an older crowd and a late bar.

Another problem with younger members was that they didn't have a lot of money to spend over the bar.

The Fix was now appearing twice a week and had a big following. Other groups continuing to make regular appearances included The Escorts, Cy Tucker, The Runaways, The Hillsiders, The Detours, The Notions, Jason Eddie, The Twig, the Connoisseurs, The Calderstones; all of these groups were reliable and well presented.

The Concordes made their club debut Sunday 18th December. Jim Whitfield, who played guitar with the group, appeared at many city venues, The Cavern, The Beachcomber, The Downbeat, The Fourwinds and The Pyramid, but playing at the Mardi Gras was always special.

Saturday 24th, Christmas Eve, last appearance by The Hillsiders. A very professional and well-presented group but Country music was not what our members wanted. I gave the news to Joey Butler who was a good friend of many years from our time as boy scouts in Mossley Hill.

1967

The practice of asking for birth certificates continued but not without its hiccups. With the boys it was a lot easier to knock back the under 18s but with the girls when they had their make-up on it was not so easy. Borrowing membership cards was another problem. For example, Maureen Leatham from Bowring Park got the loan of a card from a friend; the Mardi was her favourite club. Travelling into town on the bus with a friend they would practise repeating the name, address and date of birth on the card. The door staff would stop 'members' they suspected of using borrowed cards, and quite a number had not done their homework. Another problem was people borrowing relatives' birth certificates. Christine Jamieson from West Derby was one of the many members who found romance at the club, meeting Billy Metcalf, her future husband.

Behaviour at the club was excellent without any trouble. The police with their regular visits had no cause to complain.

Friday 17th February debut for The Beachwoods.

Auditions for new groups continued on Tuesdays. They would play at the beginning of the evening for 30 minutes to give them the chance to perform within the club atmosphere. The groups that had potential and given a further booking included The Runaways, Chapter Six, Principals, Reaction, Do-Does, Tremas, First Edition, Expressions, Bentics, Phoenix Sound, Pro-Tems, Dimples, Troubles, Mistake and Becketts Kin.

Saturday 13th June the final club appearance of The Escorts.

Saturday 22nd July and a first appearance of The Undertakers. Bob Wooler and Dougie Evans were now running an agency for local groups at the Cavern. I had a meeting with them at the Cavern office to arrange an exchange of groups between both clubs, The Undertakers being the most prominent; they appeared at the Mardi on nine occasions, the final time on Friday 13th October.

Name change, The Downbeat Club re-named Victoriana

Dave Beattie was now the manager of the Downbeat and decided on change of name; from Wednesday 8th November the club would be known as the Victoriana. To celebrate this event a grand party was held for members only. The evening featured the one and only Ben E. King with The Senete, The Detours, The Beechwoods and the resident group The Vix. Admission was free.

The film *Bonnie and Clyde* had recently been released and was the subject of a real life drama in the UK. A man and his girlfriend started a series of robberies around the country. They would commit a crime and then move on. These crimes captured the imagination of the whole country with reports on national TV news.

Don Robinson, the proprietor of the Regent hotel just across the road from the club, would pop in for a social drink. He would recommend the club to any young guests. Don realised that a couple who were guests visited the Mardi on a Sunday night. The next day Don became suspicious about the couple being the UK Bonnie and Clyde and informed the police. The car they had been using was found abandoned in the carpark at the rear of the club. The BBC TV Northern News sent a cameraman and a young reporter to film the event. The cameraman, Walter McAvoy, was an old friend; I'd known Walter from my time working at the Cavern where he took many photographs of the club's early days. Walter wanted to film from an elevated position looking down on the reporter with the carpark in the background. Jimmy Leech and I came to his assistance with a rickety pair of step ladders. Jimmy and I held the ladder firm allowing Walter to climb the steps and complete the report. The young man was the local BBC TV reporter John Humphreys who went on to be a famous face on BBC TV and the presenter of the award winning BBC Radio 4 programme 'Today'; from that day I followed his career with great interest.

Walter McEvoy, BBC cameraman

I was told a few years later that Walter had been killed in a freak car accident at Oulton Park.

Saturday 23rd December debut for Fringe Benefit, a group who became very popular and made many appearances at the club.

Sunday 24th December, Christmas Eve, Three groups, Steve Aldo and The Fix who were becoming a big favourite at the club and appearing on many nights, The Detours, and The Connoisseurs. The same three groups also appeared Tuesday 26th, Boxing Night, which they appreciated with most of their equipment staying at the club.

Friday 31st December, New Year's Eve, Steve Aldo and The Fix, The Connoisseurs, yes again, and The Runaways.

1968

The club continued to be popular although losing members to clubs with a 2am licence.

Steve Aldo and The Fix became the big attraction, sometimes appearing at the club three times a week.

Saturday 27th January club debut for Curiosity Shop, other groups making their first appearance this month, Washington Soul Band, The Defenders and The Detonators.

New groups for February, Pattern People, Perfumed Garden, Stem Band, The Circulation, Hinge, The Vix who were resident at the Victoriana Club, Fact and Fiction and Cast.

With more than 400 groups on Merseyside we tried to give a booking to as many as possible. Making their first appearance in March, Fagins Cupboard, Cherished Memories, Good Times, The Huytones, Tee Bunkum Band Bee Jays and Pattern People

At the beginning of March Liverpool Corporation bus staff went on strike. Most of our members depended on public transport and private taxies were not available in any great numbers. Buses coming into Liverpool from areas outside the city boundary were not allowed to stop until the terminus in support of their striking colleges. The club lost a lot of trade. The followers of jazz would attend the club year after year but the followers of beat music were younger and the turnover in membership was shorter, resulting in a reduction of new members. Another problem was getting the staff into work and taking them home at the end of the evening – those of us who had cars had to ferry staff members each night. The strike lasted nearly 12 weeks with the buses returning to the streets of Liverpool on Monday 27th May. It was very costly to all businesses in the city centre.

MERSEYBEAT LEGENDS

THE HIDEAWAYS - pictured at the Mardi Gras Club in 1967. They appeared at the Cavern Club more than 250 times. In 1964 they were chosen to advertise Timex watches in a major TV advertisement, which can be seen on the '100 Greatest Adverts' DVD. Hideaways member Frankie Conner (centre), now a presenter for Radio Merseyside, has co-written over 70 songs (with Alan Crowley - ex Billy Butler & The Tuxedo's), which have been recorded by original Merseybeat artists for the 'Class of 64' CDs.

The Hideaways at the Mardi (Frankie Conner centre)

Friday 5th April The Platters, Steve Aldo and the Fix, with the first club appearance of The Hideaways who were an established group featuring a young Frankie Connor. They were a favourite group at the Cavern Club, having played there many times.

Friday 19th April direct from America the fantastic Ronettes, The Seftons, The Pikkins and making his Mardi debut as DJ and compere a young Billy Butler. 7:45pm to 2am admission 7/6d (with a 2am bar extension)

The American acts became a feature every other Friday and eventually every week. They would appear on stage at the Mardi at 9:30pm and at the Victoriana 11pm. Billy compered and introduced the acts at both clubs.

Friday 3rd May The Showstoppers (Aint Nothin' But a House Party), The Reaction, Good Times and Billy Butler.

Friday 17th May The fabulous Isley Brothers, The Reaction, The Defenders and Billy Butler.

The cost of the American acts was expensive but with the increase in admission prices plus the extra bar takings it was a financial success, with the club packed on each of these nights, especially considering the problems with the on-going bus strike.

Friday 31st May James Brown Junior, The Reaction, The Hideaways and Billy Butler.

Charlie and Inez Foxx

A bar extension for the Friday night was not granted automatically, it had to be considered by the magistrates to be a special occasion. I must have had an honest face being refused on just one occasion.

Sunday 2nd June club debut of the New Mojo Band.

146

Friday 14ᵗʰ June fabulous American group The Fantastics, plus The Reaction, Fagins Cupboard and Billy Butler.

Friday 28th June The Fabulous Impressions with The Hammer, also The Top, The Defenders and Billy Butler.

Tuesday 2nd July Sinbad, and making her first appearance at the club, Beryl Marsden, plus Steve Aldo and The Fix – quite a strong bill.

Friday 12ᵗʰ July a break from the American groups with the Alan Price Set appearing at the Mardi only – just as well, it took the 'roadies' over an hour to set up the stage.

Friday 26ᵗʰ July and another UK attraction Geno Washington and the Ramjam Band, plus PP's Attraction, The Top and Billy Butler.

Friday 9th August The Symbols (Best Part of Breaking Up), The Keys, Fagins Cupboard and Billy Butler.

Friday 23rd August the one and only Ben E. King plus Curiosity Shop, The Top and Billy Butler. This was one night we had to restrict the number of visitors; members would start queuing from 6:30pm. The doors would close at 8pm with an increase in admission price.

Friday 30th August fabulous American group The Fantastics plus Fragrant Blend, The Top and Billy Butler.

Friday 6th September Little Anthony and The Imperials who were a late replacement for Lee Dorsey (Ride Your

MARDI GRAS CLUB, LIVERPOOL

Pony), with support groups and Billy Butler.

Friday 20th Sly and the Family Stone… We regret that due to circumstances beyond our control Sly and the Family Stone will not be appearing tonight. On stage tonight Hi-tones, Michael Henry Group and Billy Butler, normal admission price. The reason for the American group's cancellation was due to incorrect papers to enter the UK.

Friday 27th September Tamela Motown's own Edwin Starr plus two supporting groups and Billy Butler.

Friday 4th October the Original Drifters plus two groups and Billy Butler.

Friday 11th October direct from America Ex. Drifter Clyde McPhatter plus two groups and Billy Butler.

Friday 11th October direct from America, Dionne's sister, Dee Dee Warwick plus two groups and Billy Butler.

The club continued to engage local groups Tuesday, Saturday and Sunday and for private functions. Saturday 19th October two groups appearing at the Mardi for the first time, Familiarity Breeds and Chris Carma's Road Show.

Friday 25th October The Freddie Mac Shop, plus two groups and Billy Butler.

Friday 1ˢᵗ November Charlie and Inez Foxx (Mokin Bird) plus two groups and Billy Butler. The club having restricted band room space, Charlie and Inez booked into the Shaftesbury Hotel opposite the club and arrived ready to go on stage. My office was used by the American groups as a dressing room, providing more space and the luxury of a bathroom.

Friday 8ᵗʰ November The Voice of Soul, direct from America Oscar Toney Jnr; plus Michael Henry Group, The Memories, and Billy Butler.

Sharon Tandy

Friday 15th November Atlantic Record Night featuring Sharon Tandy (come and collect your free LPs) plus Familiarity Breeds, Fresh Garbage and Billy Butler.

Friday 22nd November Garnet Mimms plus The Charge, Familiarity Breeds and Billy Butler.

Friday 29th November direct from America The Chiffons plus two groups and Billy Butler.

Friday 6th December direct from America J.J.Jackson, two groups and Billy Butler.

Friday 13th December direct from America The Original Drifters, plus Chris Carma's Road Show, Michael Henry Group and Billy Butler.

Friday 20th December Root and Jenny Jackson, plus Sinbad and Beryl Marsden, Chapter Six and Billy Butler. Sinbad and Beryl Marsden appeared four nights that week.

Friday 27th December The Bandwagon (Breaking Down The Walls of Heartache) plus two groups and Billy Butler.

1969

Friday 3rd January direct from America the Soul Brothers with Baby Mae, plus Michael Henry Group, The Memories and Billy Butler.

Tuesday 7th January members' Christmas bonus, J.B.W and the Funkey Fever, Perfumed Garden and Michael Henry Group. Normal admission prices.

We regret that due to illness Sharon Tandy will not be appearing at the club tonight.

Friday 10th January direct from America Billy 'Fat Boy' Stewart plus two groups and Billy Butler.

Friday 17th January direct from America Johnnie 'O' plus The Memories, The Inntranzit and Billy Butler.

Friday 24th January The Ferris Wheel, plus Michael Henry Group, Familiarity Breeds and Billy Butler.

The following notice appeared in the *Liverpool Echo:* 'The management of the Mardi Gras and Victoriana clubs regret that the booking of Erma Franklin has been cancelled upon receiving information that she is not the real Erma Franklin. Her place tonight will be taken by The Ferris Wheel.

Friday 31ˢᵗ January The Foundations (Build Me Up Buttercup), two groups and Billy Butler.

Tuesday 4ᵗʰ February club debut for Colonel Bagshot's Incredible Bucket Band

Friday 7ᵗʰ February hit recorders of 'Baby Come Back'

The Equals plus two groups and Billy Butler.

Friday 14th February direct from America The Vibrations plus Headline News, Familiarity Breeds and Billy Butler.

Tuesday 18th February Mardi Gras Festival Dance with Curiosity Shop, Familiarity Breeds and Billy Butler.

Friday 21st February direct from America Horace plus The Buzzells, The Memories and Billy Butler.

Friday 28th February return visit of The Equals plus two groups and Billy Butler.

Tuesday 4th March Jimmy Ireland opens his second club in Seel Street, The Babalou.

Friday 7th March recorders of 'People' The Tymes plus two groups and Billy Butler.

Thursday 13th March after an absence of nearly three years jazz makes a return to the Mardi with the Alex Welsh Band and Merseysippi Jazz Band, tickets 7/6d plus late bar.

Billy Butler was now appearing each Tuesday night in addition to his normal Friday stint.

Friday 14th March direct from America The Topics plus two groups and Billy Butler.

THE RONETTES

Exclusive European Representation
London Attractions Ltd.
52/54 Dean Street,
London W.1.
Tel: Regent 3051

Ronettes

Friday 21ˢᵗ March the one and only Ben E.
King plus two groups and Billy Butler.

Another full house with the doors closed at 8pm, normal admission price 7/6d although we could have charged double and still filled the club...

Friday 28th March direct from America The
'G' Cleffs recorders of 'I Understand'.

Good Friday 4th April no American groups, two local groups Headline
News and Perfumed Garden, bar extension not allowed on this day.

Friday 11th April The Ronettes plus two groups and Billy Butler.

Friday 18th April from the USA 20 stone of solid soul
J.J.Jackson with The Greatest Little Soul Band plus Chris
Carma Road Show, Tomorrows People and Billy Butler

Sunday 20th April backing group for Edwin Starr and
The Vibrations from London State Express plus Perfumed
Garden; late bar until 11:30pm members 5/.

Friday 25th April from the USA the Great Soul
Master Garnett Mimms with Ellison Hogline plus
Chalk Farm, Polka Dot Train and Billy Butler.

Friday 2nd May Bob and Earl (Harlem Shuffle) with The
Mooch plus Taste of Honey, Curiosity Shop and Billy Butler.

Friday 9th May The Original Drifters plus Headline
News, Reason Why and Billy Butler.

Sunday 11th May, last appearance prior to continental
tour of Colonel Bagshot's Incredible Bucket Band.

MAGNIFICENT "MARY WELLS"

Friday 16th May, Mary Wells (My Guy) plus Acropolis, Action Line and Billy Butler. Mary Wells was eight months pregnant – the management were panicking at the thought of her going into labour.

Friday 23rd May Inez and Charlie Foxx plus Perfumed Garden, Magic Roundabout and Billy Butler.

Friday 30th May The Platters plus Curiosity Shoppe (formerly The Beechwoods), To-Morrows People and Billy Butler.

At the beginning of June I gave notice to Stan of my intention to leave my job as club manager. My parents had bought a bakery in South Liverpool. I had a financial interest in this venture but I was not in any way concerned with the working arrangements. It soon became essential that I was needed full time. I had been working at the bakery in the early mornings before going on to the club at 11am, but it soon became apparent that I couldn't manage both jobs and I would be leaving at the end of the month

Friday 6th June return visit by great demand, Bob and Earle plus Curiosity Shoppe, The Acropolis and Billy Butler.

Friday 13th June Desmond Dekker and The Aces plus Curiosity Shoppe, Action Mind and Billy Butler.

Friday 20th June The Bandwagon plus two groups and Billy Butler.

Tuesday 24th June the BBC Radio 1 lunchtime programme 12noon to 2pm broadcast live from the club. An interested spectator visiting the club for the first time, DJ John Peel.

Friday 27th June Len Barry (1, 2, 3.) plus The Dresden's, The Tridents and B.B. Phonographic Delights.

This was my last night and before the club opened the staff gathered to see me presented with an inscribed silver tankard by the management with thanks for my past services.

I had to sign papers tending my resignation as a director of Roberts and Ireland Ltd; although Jimmy Ireland no longer had any connection with the business the name of the company never altered.

Sunday 29th June Perfumed Garden, Chalk Farm plus new Elaine's Speakeasy Disco. I don't know who Elaine was. The *Echo* advertisement stated "Mardi Gras Makes Sense". When I placed advertisements in the *Echo* they were very plain and to the point without any embellishment. The word Disco was new. When I first became manager of the club records were never played. The changeover between jazz bands took less than five minutes, when the beat groups made their changeover it would take more than 10 minutes. During this silence it became necessary to fill the time with records – nothing special played on a very poor sound system.

Friday 4th July Jamo Thomas (I Spy for the F.B.I.) with Pandora's Box plus Perfumed Garden, Reason Why, Billy Butler and his Phonographic Delight.

Friday 11th July Tamela Star Jimmy Ruffin, Curiosity Shoppe, Universal Colours, Billy Butler and his Phonographic Delights.

Friday 18th July direct from America The Ronettes, Acropolis, Curiosity Shoppe and Billy Butler and his Phonographic Delights.

Sunday 20th July Elaine returns with her Speakeasy
Disco plus Chris Carma Road Show.

Friday 25th July The Freddie Mac Extravaganza, Village Band,
Familiarity Breeds and Billy Butler and his Phonographic Delights.

Sunday 27th July Elaine's Speakeasy Disco plus Curiosity Shoppe.

Friday 1st August Max Romeo.

Sunday 3rd August The Inn-Tranzit, Number
Two Sounds and guest of Number 6.

Friday 8th August The Crystals (on stage 9:30), Perfumed
Garden, Village Band and Billy Butler Phonographic Delights.

Friday 15th August Root and Jenny Jackson plus Familiarity
Breeds, Reason Why and Billy Butler Phonographic Delights.

Friday 29th August by public demand excitement unlimited,
Bandwagon (Breaking Down the Walls of Heartache), Chris
Carma Road Show, Action Line, plus Billy Butler Thing.

Sunday 31st August from BBC Radio One Club
Perfumed Garden plus Chris Wharton's Thing.

Saturday 5th September The Skatalites with the
Allsorts plus Reason Why and Billy Butler.

Tuesday 9th September Colonel Bagshot's Incredible Bucket Band. Free Membership Tuesday and Friday.

Friday 12th September The Inter-State Road Show (on stage 9:30) plus Chris Carma's Road Show, Village Band and Billy Butler's Thing.

Friday 19th September Joyce Bond Revue, Chris Carma Road Show, The Acropolis and BB's Thing.

Saturday 20th September Village Band, Allsorts and Wharton's Wheezings.

Friday 3rd October The Chants, Curiosity Shoppe, Allsorts and BB's Thing.

Friday 10th October Clarence 'Frogman' Henry plus Familiarity Breeds, Trident and BB's Thing.

Saturday and Sunday 11th & 12th October Chris Wharton's a regular spot with Wharton's Wheezings.

Friday 17th October Ben.E. King (on stage 9:30) with The Globe Show plus Village Band, Acropolis and 'Essence' of Butler. Ben.E. King always a guaranteed full house at the Mardi.

Saturday 18th October Ned Pringle, Pure Instinct and 'Whiffs' of Wharton.

Sunday 19th October from London for one night
only State Express and Number Two Sounds.

Friday 24th October The Drifters with The Clan plus
Reason Why, Allsorts and 'Essence' of Butler.

Saturday 25th October Familiarity Breeds,
Acropolis and 'Whiffs' of Wharton.

Sunday 26th October Ned Pringle and Wharton's 'Wanderings'.

Friday 31st October The Shirells (Will You Still Love
Me Forever) with Archimedes Principal plus Familiarity
Breeds, Pendulum and 'Essence' of Butler.

Tuesday 4th November The Chants, plus Skid Row, Acropolis, Toy
Town Express and BB's Thing. Members 5 shillings (25 pence).

Friday 7th November Inez and Charlie Foxx with Skid Row, Reason
Why, Acropolis, Toy Town Express and 'Essence' of Butler.

Friday 14th November The Lovin' Spoonful (What a Day For a
Daydream) plus Trident, Time Machine and 'Essence' of Butler.

Friday 21st November Fontella Bass (Rescue Me) plus
Familiarity Breeds, Pure Instinct and BB's Super Thing.

Sunday 23rd November Acropolis and orbit
with Wharton plus your free bear.

*Tuesday 25th November Sin-bad with Beryl
Marsden, also BB Super Thing and the bear.*

*Friday 28th November Marv Johnson with The Pavement,
Reason Why, Trident and BB's Super Discs.*

*Saturday 29th & Sunday 30th November Chris Wharton
continues to appear under various guises such as Wharton's
Wavelength and a bear, Wharton's Wheezings, an orbit with
Wharton and 'Whiff's' of Wharton, he's cheaper than a group!*

*Friday 5th December The Drifters with The Clan, plus
Mint, Sweet Thanks and BB's Super Disco.*

*Friday 12th December James & Bobby Purify, plus
Acropolis, Pure Instinct and BB's Super Discs.*

Tuesday 16th December The Hideaways and BB's Super Thing.

*Friday 19th December The Platters (on stage 9:30)
Sin-Bad with Poke, and BB's Super Discs.*

*Wednesday 24th December, Christmas Eve, Colonel
Bagshot's Incredible Bucket Band plus Acropolis, Cool
Cat Chris Wharton and Boppin Billy Butler.*

*Friday 26th December, Boxing Night, Cassius Butler,
Sonny Wharton, plus Perishers, Sin-Bad with Beryl
Marsden, and the rockin' Clayton Squares.*

Sunday 28th December The Hideaways plus Chris tribute to Billy.

Wednesday 31st December, New Year's Eve, Familiarity Breeds plus Mint, with grandfather Chris Wharton and 'Nappy' Billy Butler.

1970

Sunday 4ᵗʰ January Merv Johnson's backing group, The Pavement, plus Chris Wharton's Concrete Cabbage.

Tuesday 6th January Soul Seventy Series, Shuffler Sound, B.B. giving it away.

Friday 9th January The Showstoppers with Jude Brown, plus Trident and B.B. super new thing.

Sunday 11th January Confusius (formerly The Hideaways).

Friday 16th January The Chiffons with State Express, Reason Why and Pure Instinct, plus B.B. Super Discs.

Tuesday 20th January Soul 70, fantastic six piece coloured band Jason 'T' and B.B.

Friday 23rd January The Coasters with Jude Brown, plus Acropolis, Sweet Thanks and B.B. Super Discs.

Sunday 30th January the one and only Edwin Starr with The Pavement plus Pure Instinct, Storm and B.B. Super Discs.

Friday 6th February The fantastic Fantastics with The Globe Show, Trident, Toy Town Express and B.B. All Discs Super.

Sunday 8th February, free to members, Living Disco at the Mardi every Sunday.

Tuesday 10th February Shrove Soul Scene '70. All coloured super group Choice of Colours plus B.B.

Friday 13th February Red River Band plus Reason Why, National Soul Band and B.B. Phonographic Delights.

Sunday 15th February Billy and Chris DJs Fab Go, Go Girls.

Tuesday 17th February Soul Satisfaction all the Way, with that exciting new discovery Billy Butler.

Friday 20th February International hit recorders The Foundations on stage 9.30pm plus three groups and disco.

Sunday 22nd February Living disco is a gas. Tonight Gas Night, admission 1/- (5p). Fellas looking for a gas girl, meter at the Mardi. Billy, Chris and Go Go Girls

Tuesday 24th February Soul 70 Shake Down Sound plus the immaculate personality Billy Butler.

*Friday 27th February from the USA three groovy girls
hit recorders Lovers Concerto, plus Attack and The
Toys, and three groups with DJ Billy Butler.*

*Sunday 1st March Living disco packed again,
Backbreaking Special Limbo Competition. Billy and Chris,
sensational Go Go Dancers Mid-Night Movers.*

Tuesday 3rd March every Tuesday the very finest coloured soul groups.

*Friday 6th March The greatest live action group in the world The
Bandwagon on stage 9.30 pm, plus two groups and Billy Butler.*

*Saturday 7th March Barney Rubble's Booze Band,
plus Chris Wharton's sound classics.*

*Sunday 8th March Meat Meat Meat at the
famous living disco Pie Eating Contest.*

*Pies by Linford's of Aigburth Road and those mouth-
watering Jocks, Butler 'N Wharton.*

*Tuesday 10th March, Music, Music, Music
with Cleveland Fox plus BB*

*Friday 13th March from New York, The Great Ronettes
on stage 9.30pm plus Familiarity Breeds and disco.*

Saturday 14th March Top local group Reason

Why plus Chris's Music Explosion.

Tuesday 17th March, St Patricks Night, Liverpool's
tallest Leprechaun plus Billy O' Butler.

Friday 20th March James and Bobby Purify plus two groups and BB.

Sunday 22nd March Soul Scene Living Disco
Billy and Chris DJs 3 Go, Go Dancers.

Tuesday 24th March seven piece group Peaceful Soul.

Sunday 29th March Easter Sunday Living Fancy Dress event,
all in fancy dress admitted free, Billy 'N Chris 3 Go Go Girls.

Tuesday 31st March Members free, Easter
Special Spin A Soul Scene '70 with BB.

Friday 3rd April The Platters plus two groups.

Friday 10th April The Showstoppers plus Reason Why and Disco.

Sunday 12th April Living Disco Bobbin
BB, Cool Cat Chris Jiving Judies.

Friday 17th April The Liquidator is in town Harry J's All Stars.

Friday 24th April Doris Troy (Just One
Look). Barney Rubble's Booze Band.

Friday 1ˢᵗ May Ben E. King.

Friday 8th May from America The Crystals, two groups plus Disco.

*Saturday 9th May Familiarity Breeds plus
Shropshire's top DJ Darrell Jay.*

Friday 15th American hit recorders Steam.

Friday 22nd May Geno Washington and the Ram Jam Band.

Friday 5th Inex and Charlie Foxx plus Hector's House and Disco.

Friday 12th June America's Queen of Soul Carla Thomas plus BB.

*Friday 26th June The Original Drifters, now
known as The Invitations on stage 9.30pm.*

Saturday 27th June Vocal Perfection plus Liquid Heat and Joey Wall.

No name groups or acts for the summer months July and August,
the pattern of entertainment being local groups and disco featuring
BB, Chris, Darrell Jay and Joey Wall.

*Saturday 15ᵗʰ August. In appreciation of the support each Tuesday
and Saturday by our members this Saturday will be only 3/- (15pence)
for members. Fabulous London group Boundary plus Darrell Jay.*

Saturday 29th August an absolutely magnificent group six piece coloured band State Penitentiary with two coloured female vocalists.

*Saturday 18th September Valentino's on
stage at 9:15pm plus Billy Butler.*

The trend of local groups and DJs continued until the end of
November.

*Friday 27th November Johnny Johnson and
the Bandwagon on stage 9:15pm.*

*Saturday 28th November Christmas begins early at the
Mardi Gras, starting this Saturday and every Saturday
'Party Night' DJs Darrell Jay and Joey Wall.*

*Thursday 24th December, Christmas Eve Explosion,
Billy and Chris plus Familiarity Breeds.*

Thursday 31st December, New Year's Eve Disco Party, BB and CW.

1971

Friday 1ˢᵗ January, BB Hangover. *The only way to start 1971 tomorrow always ahead of our time. The M.G. announces its 1983 New Year's party.*

Saturday 2nd January Hair Night Disco, no Baldy members admitted.

No groups during January, only Disco.

Friday 5th February The Fantastics plus nine piece band.

Friday 12th February the world's top soul singer, Edwin Starr.

Sunday 14th February Living Valentine Disco, Chris (Cupid) Wharton and Billy (Oh My Aching Heart) Butler.

Friday 19th February Familiarity Breeds.

The next performance by a live band was Good Friday 9th April, The Gems plus their sensational backing group Boot Polish.

Friday 23rd April The Chants.

Friday 30th April Vocal Perfection.

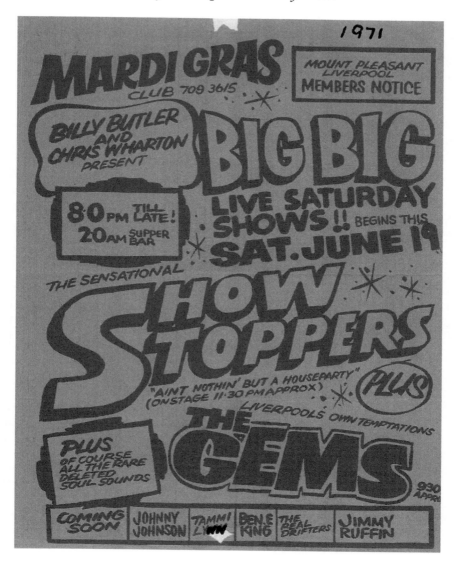

Friday 14th May The Gems.

Friday 21st May Garnet Mimms with his own eight piece band.

Friday 4th June this is the big one direct from the USA on stage 11:30pm Arthur Conley plus Vocal Perfection.

Friday 11th June England's Jackson Five State Penitentiary plus Manchester's top coloured band Merlin.

Friday 18th June eight piece coloured band Sensations.

Saturday 19th June a sensational weekend from USA, The Showstoppers on stage 11:30pm plus The Gems on stage 9:30pm.

Friday 25th June from Chicago, USA Jimmy Lewis plus White Ebony.

Saturday 26th June three groups from Jamaica, The High Timers, The Brandies and The Shades.

Friday 2nd July The Gems.

Saturday 3rd July The Gems on stage 9:30pm, Johnny Johnson and The Bandwagon on stage 11:30pm.

Friday 9th July Arthur Conley's backing group Soul Machine.

Saturday 10th July from America Tami Lynn.

Tuesday 13th July Help! An appeal from all the beautiful female members of the Mardi Gras, every Tuesday we have at the club 150 ladies and only 50 gents. It's just not right so come on, fellas, let's see more of you, we're very lonely and don't forget it's free.

Friday 16th July Greyhound on stage 11:30pm

Friday 23rd July The Fantastics.

Saturday 24th July The Gems plus Merlin.

Friday 30th July Ben E. King on stage 9:30pm.

Friday 6th August England's Jacksons Five State Penitentiary, guest DJ from Radio Luxembourg Paul Burnette, BB and CW.

Saturday 7th August The Chants.

Friday 13th August Delroy Williams Show.

Sunday 15th August Skol Drinking Competition.

Friday 20th August The Fascinations on stage 11:30pm.

Sunday 22nd August Living Disco plus Skol Drinking Competition, 10 minute time limit. Last week's winner J. Doherty six pints.

Friday 27th August The Drifters on stage 12 midnight.

MARDI GRAS CLUB, LIVERPOOL

Saturday 28th August The Gems.

Sunday 29th August Skol Drinking Competition, 10 minute drinking time. Last week's winner M Kendricks six and a half pints.

Friday 3rd September Coda Rye.

Wed 8th September Audience in concert with Galliard and Strife. Tickets 50p from Rushworth and Draper. Something new? The club was not normally open on a Wednesday or sold tickets via an agency.

Friday 17th September Edwin Starr on stage 9.30pm.

Saturday 25th September Jimmy Lewis plus funky show group Fairground.

Wednesday 29th September Liverpool Progressive Society present Stray plus Strife-Hamster. Tickets 50p, pay at the door.

Friday 1st October from Chicago USA 12 piece band Boss Effects.

Friday 8th October Tamela Motowns recorders 'Heaven Must Have Sent You!' Eligins.

Tuesday 12th October A La Mardi Gras commence Huit Heuvres Auj D'Hui Mardi La Grande Disco Avec Les Disc Jockeys Superb Billy (Pierre) Butler, Et Christophe (Jean) Wharton. Free to members.

174

*Friday 15th October from USA hit recorders of 'Hey
Girl Don't Bother Me' Tams on stage midnight.*

Friday 22nd October Jimmy Ruffin on stage midnight.

Friday 29th October King and Queen of Soul, Mac and Katie Kissoon.

Wednesday 3rd November Liverpool Progressive Society presents Lindisfarne (Fog on the Tyne) featuring tracks from the new Bob Johnson produced LP Charisima Artists. Tickets on sale at usual agencies.

Friday 5th November Jamaica's biggest sensation Winston Groovey on stage 10:30pm.

Wednesday 10th November Liverpool Progressive Society present in concert Arthur Brown's Kingdom Come. Tickets 50p.

Friday 12th November from USA William Bell on stage 12 midnight plus Vocal Perfection.

Wednesday 24th November Liverpool Progressive Society presents Hawkwind in concert.

Friday 26th November from Los Angeles, USA eight piece soul band Bloodstone on stage 10:30pm.

Saturday 27th November Liverpool Progressive Society presents Bullet and Third World War, Beggar Opera. 50p pay at the door.

Wednesday 1st December Liverpool Progressive Society presents Thin Lizzie plus Galliard. 25p pay at the door.

Friday 3ʳᵈ December The Fantastics.

Saturday 4ᵗʰ December Slade, admission 60p.

Wednesday 8ᵗʰ December Liverpool Progressive Society present Strife, plus Confuious (wheelchair rock 'n roll band) would this be the final performance at the Mardi for the former Hideaways? Admission 20p, it was also advertised as FREE.

Friday 10ᵗʰ December Arthur Conley on stage 11:30pm.

Saturday 11ᵗʰ December Keef Hartley Band who had played at the Woodstock Festival in 1969, plus Tear Gas and Strife plus and now for something completely different Professor Colmans Punch and Judy. 8pm-2am, 300 watt sound system. Tickets 75p.

Sunday 12th December Marathon 12noon to 12 midnight Rufus Thomas and Boss Effects plus Showstoppers. Tickets £1.00.

Wednesday 15th December Liverpool Progressive Society present Van Der Graaf Generator plus Clubs. Admission 50p.

Friday 17th December hit recorder Al Green with his own 10 piece orchestra. Admission 50p includes Billy and CW. We've had the paint brushes out! The Mardi is all white.

Saturday 18th December Ex Jethro Tull star Glenn Cornick with his great new band Wild Turkey plus Freedom.

Wednesday 22nd December Pre Christmas Progressive Society concert Jericho Jones plus Wave, two big groups for just 15p.

Friday 24th December, the Best Christmas Eve in Town, Vocal Perfection plus BB and CW.

Sunday 26th December, Xmas Sunday, Easter Egg with Strife plus BB and CW.

Friday 31st December Jimmy Ruffin on stage 10.30pm plus Klubbs. Jimmy Ruffin failed to appear for this booking.

1972

Saturday 1st January Amoeba plus Strife. 30p.

Sunday 2nd January Strife. 20p.

Wednesday 5th January. Every Wednesday Klubbs Guest Night plus Star guest group.

Friday 7th January The Equals (Baby Come Back) on stage 10pm. This 'gig' was poorly attended.

Saturday 8th January big name Troggy Music 'Dante' 10 piece Afro-Rock Band.

Sunday 9th January Colonel Bagshot's Incredible Bucket Band.

Wednesday 12th January The Klubbs Guest Night with, from Dublin, Skidrow.

Sunday 16th January Big Rock and Roll night,

Gus Travis and The Midnighters.

Wednesday 19th January The Klubbs Guest
Night featuring Pink Fairies.

Saturday 22nd January All Night Session Cancelled due to
circumstances beyond their control. Normal session 8pm-
2am, from London Barrabas, from Liverpool Strife.

Wednesday 26th January The Klubbs Guest Night featuring Stray.

Saturday 29th January we may not have the biggest crowd in town just
the best. Colonel Bagshot's Incredible Bucket Band plus Greasy Bear.

Wednesday 2nd February on film 93 minutes of rock
superstars plus live on stage The Klubbs.

Friday 4th February due to the lack of support from Liverpool soul
public tonight will be the last soul show here. Starting tomorrow will
become Liverpool's first heavy rock club Thursday, Friday and Sunday.

Saturday 5th February the biggest show in town three groups,
Arrival, Thin Lizzie and Barrabas, admission 50p.

Thursday 10th February 'Heavy Rock' Thursday and Friday Wild
Wally's Rock and Roll Circus plus Strife, admission only 20p.

Friday 11th February Farewell Cream, Blind Eye and Rebecca.

Saturday 12th February Heavy Rock
Saturday Little Women plus Wave.

Thursday 17th February Galliard and Moonchild, admission 20p.

Friday 18th February three groups, Pugmaho,
White Heat and Timothy, admission 30p.

Saturday 19th February Black Widow plus Strife.

Thursday 24th February Status Quo plus The Klubbs, admission 40p.

Friday 25th February three groups, Stackwaddy,
Wave and Potomac, admission 30p.

Saturday 26th February three groups, Junkyard
Angel, Mike Harrison and Amoeba.

Thursday 2nd March Greasby Bear and Timothy.

Friday 3rd March Ginger plus Moondance.

Saturday 4th March London rock band Pink Fairies plus Strife.

Thursday 9th March Gnome Sweet Gnome, Rebecca and Pussy.

Friday 10th March Hawkwind breakaway group Anon Dinn plus
Easy Street.

Saturday 11ᵗʰ March Hot Cottage and Strife, admission 40p.

Thursday 16th March Gypsy plus Galliard.

Friday 17th March Gnidrolog plus Oedipodustract.

Saturday 18th March from Scotland, Sleaze Band plus The Klubbs.

*Thursday 23rd March from Scotland, Writing
On The Wall plus White Heat.*

*Friday 24th March three groups Greasby Bear, Jerusalem
Smith and Bilbo Baggins, admission 30p.*

*Saturday 25th March Jackson Heights,
Hackensack plus DJs Billy and Chris.*

*Thursday 30th March from America Daddy
Longlegs plus Wave, admission 30p.*

Friday 31st March from Scotland, Alex Harvey Band plus Strife.

Saturday 1st April from Scotland, Tear Gas.

*Sunday 2nd April first Sunday opening since the
end of January, Tear Gas plus Strife.*

*Friday 7th April BB and CW present Liverpool's
100% Heavy Rock Club, special 20p night, Scottish*

Band, Berserk Crocodile plus Oedepodus Tract.

Saturday 8th April Galliard plus Marble Orchard, and
on film The Beatles, Little Richard and Bill Haley.

Thursday 13th April Liverpool's only 100% Heavy
Rock Centre, Pug-Ma-Ho plus Harpoon

Friday 14th April Ireland's Number 1 rock band
Thin Lizzie (paid £45) plus Possessed.

Saturday 15th April Sleaze plus Strife. On film Batman v Penguin,
Hollies, Popeye, Laurel and Hardy and George Formby.

Thursday 20th April Strife plus Madrigal, admission 20p.

Friday 21st April Argent (formed by Rod Argent
formerly of The Zombies) plus Pussy, only 60p.

Thursday 27th April Pink Fairies, plus Strife, admission 30p.

Friday 28th April Strife, Jerusalem Smith plus
Magical Mystery Tour, admission 30p.

Saturday 29th April 100% heavy rock from
Hackensack plus from London Hot Cottage plus on
film Magical Mystery Tour, admission 30p.

Thursday 4th May Pug-Ma-Ho plus Amocba, admission 20p.

Friday 5th May Scotland's number 1 Heavy Rock
Band Nazareth plus Jerusalem Smith.

Thursday 11th May two bill toppers Walrus plus Sleaze Band.
On film Winifred Atwell, Herbs and Mario Lanza.

Friday 12th May two great bands Sleaze Band
and The Klubbs plus usual goodies

Saturday 13th May Tear Gas plus Possessed.

Thursday 18th May Chicago Climax Band plus
Mammoth Tool Co; on film Al Jolson, and Robin
Hood. ASTOUNDING NEWS SOON.

Friday 19th May Liverpool's premier big name
Thin Lizzie plus on stage 9.30pm Fly.

Saturday 20th May Audience plus The Klubbs, films and disco.

Thursday 25th May from London great rock 'n roll band featuring
former Grease Band Memphis Bend plus Strife, admission 20p.

Thursday 1st June Closing Down Due To Demolition Order.
Don't miss our final three sessions. D-Day minus 2. He's here,
the arch-looner rockin' ex. Jethro Tull, Bloodwin Pig, Mick
Abrahams Band plus Flying Hat Band, admission 30p.

Friday 2nd June D-Day minus 1, two great groups for our

last Friday, Tear Gas plus The Klubbs admission 35p.

Saturday 3rd and Sunday 4th June gigantic closing show 8pm to very late. Nine groups, Roy Young Band, Thin Lizzie, Sleaze Band, Greasy Bear, Galliard, Tear Gas, Strife, Klubbs, Bilf Splatt.

Billy and Chris on stage at the Mardi

Plus the world's most underrated rhubarb turners, the heartbroken William George Butler, Christopher Francis Wharton. No admission after 1am.

Due to impatient progressive bulldozers to-nite is our final session, we're being flattened Monday.

Carol and Roy Young recall the final night at the club with wall to wall people you could hardly move, plastic or foam cups. "We topped the bill on the final nearly night; Chris sent the final night programme and a copy of the contract, which we still possess from agent Robert Stigwood. I think the club was torn down the following Monday."

Roy who is nearly as old as me has been around in the Rock 'n Roll business since the early 1950s. His trade mark boogie-woogie piano and vocal style was described as a mixture between Little Richard, Ray Charles and Joe Cocker. He played in Germany in the 1960s with Tony Sheridan and Ringo Starr. He has recently released a double CD, Roy Young –the Best of 50 Years.

Billy and Chris had continued to book bands in the hope that the demolition order would be delayed and signed contracts with Wild Turkey to appear on Thursday 8th June for a fee of £60 or 60% of the door entrance fee; Gypsy were booked to appear for Thursday 15th June for £60 or 60%. Vinegar Joe was due to appear on Thursday 22nd June for £75 or 60%. This band featured Salford born singer Elkie Brooks and Robert Palmer. The contracts for these gigs were signed in April and May.

An announcement in the *Liverpool Echo* Monday 5th June:

'Billy Butler and Chris Wharton would like to thank all the members of the Mardi Gras for their tremendous support and enthusiasm. You are the best crowd we have ever worked for in twelve years in the business. See you all at our new scene soon. Many thanks Virgen and Probe, Roger Eagles, Strife, Klubbs, Bob McGrave, and the Bloots for past help.'

The building, along with other properties on that side of Mount Pleasant, was demolished a short time later to make way for a multi-storey car park and a place of entertainment on the Mardi site.

The building which was built as a place of religious worship in the late 18th century would now close and would be demolished after nearly 200 years, as a place of music worship. Stan Roberts and Jimmy Ireland have never received the recognition they richly deserved for their contribution to the Liverpool 60s music scene.

The Victoriana club advertisement in the *Liverpool Echo* Wednesday 7th June:

'Freakies, Weirdies, Hairies and Heads. Mardi Gras R.I.P. The Vic goes heavy every Thursday and Saturday. This Thursday, Confucious. All ex. Vic and Mardi members welcome

The memories of Chris Wharton

After Brian's departure John Egerton became the club manager. John, whose basic trade was that of bookkeeper, had little knowledge of the music business. Stan and John then relied on local DJ Billy Butler to organise the groups and music content. One idea introduced being a DJ booth within the dance floor; this was not a success.

I was a friend of Billy's and had experience as a local entertainment manager with a group called The Deesiders who had played three times with the Silver Beatles at Neston Institute in 1960 and had booked The Beatles on three occasions to play at Barnston Women's Institute in 1962. I continued as an entertainment agent, booking local groups and working for the Cavern Agency for a short period.

I teamed up with Billy Butler in 1966 promoting venues at Carlton Club, Warrington, The Paradise Club, Wigan, Quantways, Chester, The Capital Ballroom, Wallasey and the Last Inn Hengeod, Oswestry.

With the attendance at the Mardi dwindling Billy and I became more involved in making decisions about what should happen. Stan and John seemed happy to go along with this arrangement. Basically we turned the place into a full Disco scene with live music from local bands and American Soul guests. The Wigan Casino had become recognised as a major rare soul record venue in the north. Billy being an avid record collector of soul music with a superb knowledge helped the Mardi to become another major Northern soul venue.

American bands doubled with Wigan and the Mardi. Wigan having the early spot at 9pm, we had a few nail biting times hoping they would arrive in Liverpool to go on stage at 11:45pm. Edwin Starr, The Drifters, Tami Lynn, The Elgins etc. all appeared on time at the Mardi and it eventually became recognised as the major soul venue in Liverpool even though the Cavern Club was also majoring with American soul acts.

The combination of good local bands, exceptional soul music via discotheque and top US artistes made the Mardi buzz. The club's big stage helped when the American acts were backed by 8 to 10 piece bands.

During this period we promoted a local band Vocal Perfection who eventually changed their name to the Real Thing and became famous with hit records 'You To Me Are Everything' and 'Can't Get By Without You'.

At the beginning of 1971 Stan came up with a proposition to sell the club to me and Billy with the goodwill, fixtures and fittings for

£1500. The partners decided that although the life of the building was unknown, paying the Council on a week to week basis was an advantage. We knew that the Council had plans to build a carpark behind the club but required one corner of the building to complete their plans. We considered it was worth the gamble. Stan had lost interest in the club and very rarely visited the premises, now and again James Roberts (Stan's son) would pop in but didn't seem interested in the place.

John Egerton continued as manager, being our supervisor and with his co-operation we kept the place going and although we wanted John to continue in his role he decided to leave in March 1971. Another long serving member of the staff, Albert Lowe, continued to work, looking after the brewery deliveries and the bars, an excellent worker and genuine guy who stayed with us for which we were grateful.

We now had full control of the place. One of the first alterations we made was to build a DJ box in the middle of the balcony and operate from there.

A trip to Amsterdam to buy some records, which was a good city for record collectors, and whilst there we paid a visit to a famous club, The Paradiso, which was basically a heavy rock live music venue but also included movies screened over the stage while bands played. In addition liquid light shows were a feature.

We returned to Liverpool and decided to copy The Paradiso as the Mardi was tailor-made for these features, having a big screen down each side wall adjacent to the dance floor. We made a screen over the stage and obtained a 16mm sound projector, already having a substantial PA/sound system we managed to find a firm in Coventry who could supply all sorts of films including Batman, many rock and roll films and even a Beatles TV show. We employed two guys from Liverpool University to do light shows on the two side walls.

By November with attendances falling we decided to drop soul music and in the New Year change to heavy rock. In December with anticipation of the change to heavy rock we painted the club all white.

In January 1972 we started what would be the best period of our Mardi Gras experience. We had a guy from Birkenhead set up a record stall, liquid lights on the two walls and films over the stage, along with some top heavy rock bands of the period. The atmosphere was incredible and no one had a venue doing the same type of thing, certainly not in Liverpool and maybe the rest of Northern England.

We were able to hire the top rock 'n roll films from the fifties and pick out the songs from famous artistes like Eddie Cochran etc. and play them as records along with normal discs during the 20 minute break when the groups were changing over. Other films included Laurel and Hardy and Batman all sent from Coventry via British Rail Red Star service to Lime Street station.

We had some strong bands appearing during the next six months including Status Quo, Thin Lizzie, Slade and Lindisfarne. The programme created some fear among the other venues such as the

Cavern Club and the Stadium.

By June 1972 it was all over. The Council to their credit had allowed us to stay as long as possible but it was time to get out. It was so sad that a potentially listed building, nearly 200 years old, was to be demolished along with one of the true historic music venues in the city, to be replaced by some horrendous carpark building.

We had an all-nighter on the last night, 3rd June, something that had been avoided until now because of police objection, but now it didn't matter and the Mardi certainly went out in style with the Roy Young Band and Thin Lizzie, along with six other bands giving us a fine farewell. Everything is now, more than 45 years on, centred on the Cavern – the Mardi Gras gets very little publicity.

It was a major northern jazz venue featuring the country's top jazz bands of the era, and the first licensed live music venue. Sadly the emphasis now is on the Beatles and anything connected with them and consequently the phoney Cavern now in existence is what tourists want to see.

The Demolition

On Monday 5th June the demolition men arrived to demolish the place, a major part of the Liverpool music scene disappearing forever. Jimmy Leech sitting in his parked car at the rear of the premises watched with great sadness as the demolition contractors started to knock down the building. This place, which had not only been his place of work but also his home for seven years. He noticed the wallpaper that he used to decorate a bedroom – it obviously meant very little to the workmen who were just doing their job but to Jimmy it was an important part of his life disappearing in a cloud of dust. It's called progress. The end of an era for Liverpool music with many varied types from traditional and modern jazz, skiffle, Merseybeat, country, soul, and heavy rock, for nearly 14 years the biggest and most successful club of the period.

Billy Butler, writing in his book '*Billy Butler MBE*', states: 'The big chance came when I was working at the Mardi Gras doing soul nights with my business partner Chris Wharton, and we were offered the chance to take over the club, which we did. We continued with the soul music but unfortunately we had a lot of trouble and had to abandon it, and use instead what we called progressive groups.'

The Mardi played a big part of my life; I met and married my wife Jean, and my three children Helen, Moira and Andrew were born during this period. When I left I became a successful Master Baker with three shops in South Liverpool. I attended the Bakery School in Colquitt St, obtaining my City and Guilds. It was a complete change to my working life, getting out of bed early rather than arriving home in the early hours of the morning. The bakery was hard work, leaving very little time to socialise. I won many prizes for my bread at exhibitions up and down the country. The business closed in 1989.

Jean sadly died of breast cancer 23rd July 1983 at the age of 41. Her friends, who would meet every Thursday for nibbles, a natter and maybe a drop of wine, were very upset by the loss of their friend and they decided to start a Memorial fund in her name. A number of fundraising events were organised including one attended by Mike McCarthy, whose mother Mary died of the same illness; he did a reading from a book of poetry he had just written.

The fund raised £10,000, enough to buy a piece of equipment for the early detection of breast cancer. This was presented to the Royal Liverpool Hospital in December 1985.

Rose Leech, who was very friendly with Jean, died six months later in January 1984 after a fall at home and is buried in Kirkdale Cemetery Longmoor Lane, Liverpool.

The End.